101对 汉英常用谚语对照

101 Pairs of Chinese-English Common Sayings

王晓钧 编著
By Xiaojun Wang Ph. D.

北京语言大学出版社
BEIJING LANGUAGE AND CULTURE UNIVERSITY PRESS

图书在版编目（CIP）数据

101 对汉英常用谚语对照/王晓钧编著. —北京：北京语言大学出版社，2008.2

书名原文：101 Pairs of Chinese-English Common Sayings

ISBN 978-7-5619-2023-7

Ⅰ.1… Ⅱ.王… Ⅲ.英语-谚语-汉、英 Ⅳ.H313.3

中国版本图书馆 CIP 数据核字（2008）第 016336 号

书　　名：101 对汉英常用谚语对照
责任印制：汪学发

出版发行：北京语言大学出版社
社　　址：北京市海淀区学院路 15 号　邮政编码：100083
网　　址：www.blcup.com
电　　话：发行部　82303650/3591/3651
编辑部　82303647
读者服务部　82303653/3908
网上订购电话　82303668
客户服务信箱　service@blcup.net
印　　刷：北京中科印刷有限公司
经　　销：全国新华书店

版　　次：2008 年 5 月第 1 版　2008 年 5 月第 1 次印刷
开　　本：787 毫米×1092 毫米　1/16　**印张**：15.25
字　　数：254 千字　　**印数**：1—3000
书　　号：ISBN 978-7-5619-2023-7/H·08012
定　　价：38.00 元

目录
CONTENTS

前言

如果说人类语言丰富绚丽，如同那多姿多彩的大海，那么蕴涵其中的民间谚语就像那晶莹闪烁的颗颗明珠。无论哪种语言都有不少谚语以口笔相传的形式流传于世。谚语听起来真切易懂，说起来朗朗上口，回味起来受益无穷。它们既是人民生活经验的提炼，又是民族智慧的结晶，同时也是语言与文学中不可缺少的部分。

汉语和英语中都有丰富多彩的民间谚语。尽管语言和文化不同，但是两种语言中的不少谚语竟好像出自同一源头。比如，汉语的"趁热打铁"与英语的"strike while the iron is hot"就有异曲同工之妙。正所谓"路有千条，理只一个"，不同民族的人民往往会用不同的语言来表达他们对生活的共同经验和感受。如果学习者能够把自己母语中的谚语与目的语中相对应的表达联系起来，那么不仅可以增强对所学谚语的理解，找到它们之间的相同点与区别，而且能提高兴趣，加深对不同语言文化的理解，并做到运用自如。

有鉴于此，本书在编写方法上进行了新的尝试。编者在对搜集整理的数千条英、汉谚语进行归类的基础上，将英、汉两种语言中反映近似哲理的谚语作了对照比较，从中精选了101对英、汉意义相近或相关的谚语，分对列出，加注词语解释，提供真实用例，以期使学习者对各条谚语在真实语境中如何使用有所了解，并能在交际中正确运用，举一反三，从而迅速提高外语表达能力。在注释方面，编者针对学习者不同的语言背景，每一条谚语不仅用读者母语加以解释说明，而且还用简明的对话方式表明具体情景和用法，并通过摘抄例句的方式提供已发表作品中的典型用例，以便于模仿使用。为了帮助理解与记忆，增强趣味性，所有谚语还配有插图。从学习者的角度讲，把英、汉意思相近的谚语列在一起，不仅可以互相参照，互为注脚，而且可以避免按字面翻译而造成的生涩难懂的困扰以及由于文化差异而产生的隔阂。学习者也会自然而然地把自己的母语与目的语联系起来，对目的语中谚语的意思和表达法心领神会，达到融会贯通的效果。

为了便于读者查找，书前、书末分别附有拼音索引和英文索引。为了方便读者，很多谚语条目下面还提供了与其意思相近或相关的其他谚语，以供参考。这样，读者可以按谚语表达的意思进行归类，在近似语义的谚语中找出最贴切的谚语来表达自己的意思（参见【参】）。很多谚语在流传使用中，也出现了一些不同形式和表达方法，读者可参见【异】项来选择使用这些谚语的不同表达形式。

对于正在学习英语或汉语的读者，掌握目的语中传统而地道、精练而生动的语句和表达法无疑是十分必要的。不言而喻，谚语的学习对提高外语水平与表达能力不但很重要，而且往往可以收到事半功倍的效果。对于那些对异国文化、民俗、社会感兴趣的人来说，通过谚语的学习与欣赏，也可以窥视到异国的风土人情，感受到异国文化的魅力，领略外国人民的智慧。对外语教师、语言研究者、文学爱好者和哲学工作者而言，本书也具有一定的参考价值。“明珠放到哪里都闪光”，各类读者一定会在语言的海洋中发现并拾取到更多的语言明珠。

王晓钧

Preface

A proverb, in Chinese, English or other languages, is a common saying with words of advice or warning. In order to become popular and memorable, it has not only to be succinct, but also imply wisdom. Proverbs, as the Dutch say, are the daughters of experience. They are expressions of significant thoughts and are the crystallizations of universal truths. Proverbs are also widely used by people to "provide the sauce to relish the meat of ordinary speech."[1] They become an integral part of a language and literature.

There are many rich and colorful proverbs, traditional or modern, in both Chinese and English. Even though their origins and language forms are different, it seems that some proverbs are related to each other, since popular wisdom over a vast variety of subjects is common to all cultures and countries. Therefore, it is possible to compare and pair them up based on their meanings. For example, 趁热打铁 in Chinese and *strike while the iron is hot* in English have different tunes but the same wisdom. If we can relate a proverb in our mother tongue to the corresponding expression in a foreign language with similar thought and application, it will be helpful for us to understand the meaning of the proverb, increase our motivation and interest to learn, enhance memory and have a good command of it in the form of the target language. However, it is important to remember that the usage of a proverb in one language could differ from the paired one in the other language.

This handbook is a collection of 101 pairs of Chinese-English proverbs based on comparison and analysis over thousands of proverbs in both languages. Each pair of the Chinese-English proverbs reflects similar everyday experience and popular wisdom with memorable forms. In order to help both Chinese language learners and English learners, each pair of the Chinese-

---

1 J. A. Simpson, (eds.) (1982) *The Concise Oxford Dictionary of Proverbs.* Oxford University Press.

English proverbs is listed together with literal translations and explanations in the learners' native language. Since many of the proverbs have oral traditions and reflect the genius of language as used by the common people, the conversational examples are provided for the users to see how those proverbs are used by native speakers in real-life situations. In addition, the included illustrative quotations establish evidence for each proverb's present value, although many of the proverbs perhaps were in common oral use before being written down. An illustration is also included to make the learning and reading a fun experience, and to increase users' interest in the proverbs. It is our intention to see each pair of Chinese-English proverbs will be easily assimilated by the readers.

Proverbs are generally listed in two ways: Alphabetical sequence and thematic presentation. To be user-friendly, this handbook orders paired proverbs in straight alphabetical sequence based on *pinyin.* An index of English proverbs paired with Chinese proverbs is also provided at the back of the book. As a result of proverbs' metaphorical application and oral tradition, many proverbs are widely different in form and/or wording, but have very similar meanings. This is a reflection of the proverbs' vitality. For those proverbs to confer with the listed ones, please see 【参】 in the English proverb section and/or 【*Cf.*】 in the Chinese section. It can be also used as the thematic category, since most of those proverbs are grouped with similar application for their essential meanings. For those proverbs that vary in wording from the listed ones, please see 【异】 and/or 【*Var.*】 in either the English or the Chinese section. Those are the varied forms of the same proverb.

This handbook can serve several purposes. For foreign language learners, it will be a very effective way to learn and use proverbs in the target language to make their speech more concise, expressive and impressive. For language instructors, linguists and writers, it can be used as a reference book. For those who are interested in foreign languages, cultures and societies, it can provide fruitful resources for them to catch glimpses of the foreign cultures, local customs and popular wisdoms through those proverbs.

使用说明

1 本书正文的谚语条目按汉语拼音顺序排列。汉语谚语均加注拼音。英语的对应条目排列在相应的汉语条目之后。

2 在书末有按英语字母顺序排列的谚语索引。汉语对应条目排列在英语条目后，共同组成一对谚语。

3 汉语谚语条目的字义、直译和解释等用英语斜体缩略语标出，以便于母语为英语的汉语学习者查阅。如：

Voc. = Vocabulary
Lit. = Literal translation
Exp. = Explanation
Ex. = Example
Quot. = Quotation
Cf. = Confer
Var. = Variation

4 英语谚语条目的直译、解释、用例等用缩略语在鱼尾号【】中标出，以便于母语为汉语的英语学习者查阅。如：

【义】=直译
【解】=意译
【例】=用例
【引】=引例
【参】=参见
【异】=异体

User's Guide

1 The Chinese-English proverbs of the text are arranged in alphabetic order of *pinyin* in this book. The pronunciation of each Chinese proverb is spelled out by *pinyin*. Each corresponding English proverb is listed under the Chinese proverb as a pair.

2 An index of English proverbs paired with Chinese proverbs is provided at the back of this book. Each corresponding Chinese proverb is listed under the English proverb as a pair.

3 The list of abbreviations related to vocabulary, literal translation, explanation, etc. on each Chinese proverb is given in italics for Chinese learners whose native language is English. For example:

Voc. = Vocabulary
Lit. = Literal translation
Exp. = Explanation
Ex. = Example
Quot. = Quotation
Cf. = Confer
Var. = Variation

4 The list of abbreviations related to literal translation, explanation, examples, etc. on each English proverb is given in【 】for English learners whose native language is Chinese. For example:

【义】=直译
【解】=意译
【例】=用例
【引】=引例
【参】=参见
【异】=异体

拼音索引
Index of Pinyin

B

G

H

J

L

M

N

101对

汉英常用谚语对照

101 Pairs of Chinese-English Common Sayings

Bāozi yǒu ròu bú zài zhěr shang

包子有肉不在褶儿上

Voc. 包子 steamed stuffed bun，肉 meat，褶儿 pleat

Lit. The steamed bun with meat stuffing doesn't necessarily have pleats.

Exp. Don't draw a conclusion about someone or something just from the appearance.

Ex. 甲：你觉得我新买的手机怎么样？

乙：不怎么样。

甲：为什么？你看它样子多漂亮啊！

乙：有句话说：包子有肉不在褶儿上。外表漂亮的手机不一定质量就好，就一定好用。

Quot. 你不用装穷，包子有肉不在褶子上……（浩然《金光大道》）

Cf. 好马不在铃铛响，好茶不在颜色浓/才人无貌，烂扇子多风/香花不一定好看，好人不一定漂亮/酒香不怕巷子深

Var. 包子好吃不在褶儿上/有肉不在褶面上

Don't judge a book by its cover

【义】不要根据一本书的封面来判定它的好坏。

【解】比喻不要单凭一些事情的表面现象来下结论。

【例】A：What do you think of our new teacher?

B：I think he will be a very tough teacher. I'll bet we'll have a hard time in his class. He seems to be the type of person who will be very strict without patience.

A：Why do you think so?

B：I guess because he seems so serious, and he seldom smiles.

A：I think you can't really tell about somebody or something based on appearance alone. **Don't judge a book by its cover**. Actually, some of my friends who took his class last semester told me that he was very kind and knowledgable.

【引】"Have you seen the new guy they hired as the coach of Commodore High's football team? He's so short and puny..." "Listen, Pal. Don't judge a book by its cover. From what I hear, that guy is one of the best."

(H. Collis, *101 American English Proverbs*, 1992)

【参】Appearances are deceptive. / All that glitters is not gold. / Still waters run deep. / Looks often deceive. / Beauty is only skin-deep. / Never choose your women or your linen by candle light. / There's many a good cook come out of a tattered bag. / There's many a good tune played on an old fiddle. / Looks aren't everything. / Don't judge everyone by his looks. / Don't judge a tree by its bark.

【异】Never judge a book by its movie. / You can't judge a book by its binding. / You can never tell a book by its cover.

Běn mò dào zhì, shì dé qí fǎn

本末倒置，适得其反

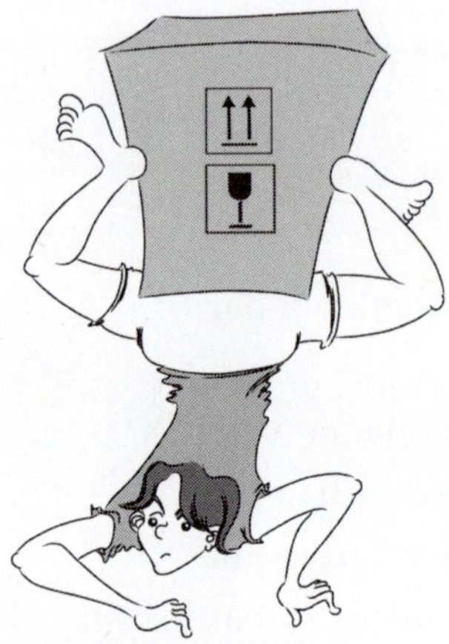

Voc. 本 root，末 branch，倒置 upside down，适 just，反 contrary

Lit. take the branch for the root

Exp. put things in the wrong position — implying doing things must follow procedures, and sense of priorities is important

Ex. 甲：妈妈，你知道吗？我终于找到我喜欢的工作了！

乙：太好了。什么时候开始上班？

甲：明天。我明天早上一定早点儿起床，好好儿打扮一下。您看，我已经买了五六套衣服，不知道穿哪套好。

乙：刚开始上班，最要紧的是工作而不是穿戴。本末倒置会适得其反。公司请你是去工作，而不是去当时装模特儿。

Quot. 该简者你却详而不简，该详者而你又简而不详。本末倒置，批评你还不愿意！（曲波《林海雪原》）

Cf. 逆风点火自烧身/砍柴不照纹，累死砍柴人/会使车，不离辙/捡了芝麻，丢了西瓜/眉毛胡子一把抓

Var. 舍本逐末，适得其反/舍本问末，适得其反

Don't put the cart before the horse

【义】不要把拖车放在马的前头。

【解】做任何事都要按照一定的次序或规则。

【例】A：Hey, Dad, guess what? I got hired for that job I was telling you about.

B：That's great! When do you start?

A：Tomorrow morning. The boss told me I'm just the girl they've been looking for.

B：I bet you you'll be a manager before too long.

A：I hope so.

B：In the meantime just remember：**Don't put the cart before the horse**. A horse can pull a cart but cannot push one very effectively. You have to keep the proper order and then you may succeed. Don't forget that first you are an employee, later on you may become a manager. It is important to do things in the right order.

【引】Sheila is putting the cart before the horse. She bought two tickets for the concert, but she hasn't yet asked her husband if he would like to come.
(*NTC's Dictionary of Proverbs and Clichés*, 1993)

【参】Put first things first. / First things first. / Which came first, the chicken or the egg?

【异】Never put the cart before the horse. / Don't get the cart before the horse. / Don't get the carriage before the horse.

Bù dāngjiā bù zhī cháimǐ guì

不当家不知柴米贵

Voc. 当家 manage the house，柴米 rice and firewood (daily necessities)

Lit. You won't know that the daily necessities are expensive until you've managed the house.

Exp. You won't know the hardship of life until you've tried to do it yourself.

Ex. 甲：妈妈，我们班不少同学都买了新电脑，我也想买一台。

乙：等过年的时候再说吧。最近家里经济情况不富裕，还要给你交学费。

甲：你不是天天都在工作吗？怎么还缺钱？

乙：不当家不知柴米贵。你将来成家了就知道过日子不容易了。

Quot. 不当家不知柴米贵，创家立业是不容易……（梁斌《播火记》）

Cf. 不生孩子不知腰酸肚子疼/站着说话不腰疼/事非经过不知难

Var. 不当家不知柴米贵，不养儿不知父母恩/不当家不晓得柴米贵/不当家不知油盐贵

Don't judge a man until you've walked in his boots

【义】你穿过一个人的靴子走路以后再来评价他走的路。

【解】表示在没有亲身体验过别人所做的事以前，不要急于去评价或批评。

【例】A：I don't like the man in our office. He got transferred in here from out-of-state, and he doesn't know how to do his job. He doesn't seem to be willing to try and get along with anyone.

B：Did you invite him to lunch or out for a coffee? Have you spent any time with him outside of work? Do you really know him at all?

A：No. I guess not.

B：**Don't judge a man until you've walked in his boots**. The first year of a new job is always the hardest. I think you shouldn't criticize a person unless you've had the same experiences.

【引】Look. Don't judge a man until you've walked in his boots. You've probably never tried to do the thing he was doing. (H. Collis, *101 American English Proverbs*, 1992)

I think it made me tolerant. It's like the old cliche: You have to walk a mile in someone else's shoes before you can really see how they like. (*New York Times*, 1992)

【参】Judge not, that ye be not judged. / Live and let live.

【异】Don't judge a man until you have walked a mile in his boots.

Bú jiàn gāoshān, bù zhī píngdì

不见高山，不知平地

Voc. 高山 high mountain，平地 flat ground

Lit. Only by seeing a high mountain can one really understand what a flat ground is.

Exp. Only by comparing can we distinguish the difference between two things.

Ex. 甲：你听说了吗？小李已经拿到博士学位了，而且他的博士论文还获了奖。

乙：是吗？几年前我们还是大学同学，他这几年进步真快。

甲：可不是嘛。不见高山，不知平地。现在我们已经落伍了。

乙：没关系，和那些没上过大学的比，我们还算不错的呢。

Quot. 不见高山，不见平地，这一来，越显得他是个能员，吴游击是个饭桶了。(《官海》，第二十四回)

Cf. 不怕不识货，就怕货比货/山高显云低

Var. 若无高山，怎显平地/没有高山，不显平地/不登高山，不现平地/不见高山，不显平地/不见高山，哪知平地/不登高山，不见平地

The greater the sinner, the greater the saint

【义】罪人的罪孽越深重，圣人就显得越伟大。

【解】比喻事物是相比较而言。没有坏就显不出好，没有平凡就显不出伟大。

【例】A：Did you know Doug is a minister now?

B：No kidding，I can't believe it. He always liked to party and have a good time. He was a wild man.

A：I know some of the trouble he was in，and I would never have expected him to become a minister. I guess **the greater the sinner，the greater the saint**.

B：I suppose some people have to live a crazy life before they settle down and lead calmer lives.

A：Amazing，isn't it?

【引】How well is the old proverb illustrated in this foul seducer... "The greater the sinner，the greater the saint."（E. Hinchcbiffe，*Barthomley*，1856）

Well，I always heard it's the biggest devils that make the best saints，and now I can believe it!（M. Lavin，*Stories I*，1964）

【参】A great city，a great loneliness. / The greater a man's reputation，the greater the criticism. / The greater the man，the greater the crime. / The greater the truth，the greater the libel.

Bù jīng yí shì, bù zhǎng yí zhì
不经一事，不长一智

Voc. 经 go through，智 wisdom

Lit. Wisdom won't grow without going through that issue.

Exp. Out of experience comes wisdom. We learn by our experiences including mistakes.

Ex. 甲：听说你在美国留学的时候开车吃了不少罚单。

乙：那算什么？谁没吃过罚单呀！再说，不经一事，不长一智。我现在开车就比以前强多了……

甲：别吹了。你看，警察让你停车呢！

乙：真倒霉，就顾着跟你说话，忘了看红绿灯了。

甲：看来，你今天又要"经一事，长一智"了。

Quot. 我认为什么本领也不是凭空得来的。俗话说得好："不经一事，不长一智。"……不下水，一辈子也不会游泳；不扬帆，一辈子也不会操船。（曲波《林海雪原》）

Cf. 实践出真知/抓鱼要下水，伐木要入林/亲自下河知深浅，亲口尝梨知酸甜/撮药三年会行医

Var. 吃一堑，长一智

Experience is the best teacher

【义】经验是最好的老师。

【解】人们往往从实际经验中学到真知，其中包括成功的经验和失败的教训。

【例】A：How did you enjoy studying in China?

B：I loved it! I improved my Chinese fluency, and learned more about the culture and the people.

A：That is wonderful! **Experience is the best teacher.**

B：I could never have learned from others what I learned by actually traveling to the country.

A：It sounds like your experiences in China taught you a lot, and you will never forget them.

【引】Experience is a hard teacher because she gives the test first, the lesson afterwards. (*This Week*, 1960)

【参】Experience is the mother of wisdom. / Wise men learn by other men's mistakes. / If it is a fault, it is no wonder.

【异】Experience is the only teacher. / Experience is a hard master but a good teacher. / Experience teaches us many things.

Bú pà yí wàn, jiù pà wànyī

不怕一万，就怕万一

Voc. 怕 afraid，一万 ten thousand，万一 in case

Lit. not be afraid of ten thousand times but once.

Exp. always be careful and be prepared for imminent dangers or exceptions

Ex. 甲：要升学考试了，你复习得怎么样？

乙：我找老师谈过，他说我的基础好，应该没问题。我猜想考试也不会太难。

甲：你最好还是好好儿复习一下。不怕一万，就怕万一。万一考不好，找老师一万次也没用。

Quot. 想来想去，他还担心……不怕一万，就怕万一。万一要有个什么闪失呢？（张俊彪《省委第一书记》）

Cf. 凡事预则立/防患于未然/没事常思有事/宁信其有，不信其无

Var. 不怕一万，只怕万一/不怕一万，单怕万一

Forewarned is forearmed

【义】预先警告就是预先做好准备。

【解】凡是预先做好最坏的准备，往往可以把事情办得更好。

【例】A：I was speaking with our English teacher recently. He said we will be discussing a book over the first few classes. Have you ever read the book?

B：No, I haven't. It won't be hard to understand, I guess.

A：Maybe you should read it over vacation. It isn't difficult if we are familiar with it. Better to read it now than when school starts and you are too busy. **Forewarned is forearmed**, you know.

B：That's true. A warning in advance gives one the opportunity to prepare for adversity.

【引】I'm pleased to share your holiday safety advice with my readers, forewarned is forearmed. (A. V. Buren, *Times*, 1994)

【异】Forewarned, forearmed. / Forewarned is quite often forearmed. / To be forewarned is to be forearmed.

Bú rù hǔ xué, yān dé hǔ zǐ

不入虎穴，焉得虎子

Voc. 入 enter，虎穴 tiger's den，焉 how can，虎子 cub

Lit. One can't get a tiger cub without entering the tiger's den.

Exp. If you dare not take risks, you will never accomplish anything (often referring to dangerous tasks).

Ex. 甲：你申请报考研究生了吗？明天报名就截止了。

乙：我知道，可是我还没申请呢！

甲：怎么搞的？

乙：我真不知道该怎么办。想试试，又怕考不上。

甲："不入虎穴，焉得虎子"。要是你什么都不敢，你就什么也做不成。如果不申请，你永远也不会知道有没有被录取的希望。

Quot. 不入虎穴，焉得虎子？……俺宋江不到东京看灯，怎晓得御屏上写下名字？（《二刻拍案惊奇》第四十卷）

Cf. 舍不了孩子打不了狼/不顶千里浪，哪来万斤鱼/胆小没有将军做

Var. 不入虎穴抱不出虎子，不闯龙潭掏不出龙蛋/不钻老虎洞，逮不住虎娃子/不入虎穴，捉不住虎子/不入虎穴，不得虎子

Nothing ventured, nothing gained

【义】venture 冒险，gain 获得

【解】如果一个人不敢冒风险就什么事也做不成。

【例】A：Hey, Daniel, how are things going?

B：Not so well. The big dance is tomorrow night and I still don't have anyone to go with.

A：I thought you were going to ask Stephani to the dance. What happened?

B：I guess I lost my nerve. I'd like to ask her, but I keep wondering if she'll accept my invitation or not.

A：Well, you know the old saying: **Nothing ventured, nothing gained**, don't you? If you don't take a risk now, you'll never gain anything. You'll never know how she feels about you if you don't ask her out.

【引】"Let me be perfectly frank — I see no point in false modesty — I am the right man for the job." ... "Well, nothing ventured, nothing gained, ah?" (M. Korda, *The Fortune*, 1989)

【参】Who dares nothing need hope for nothing. / You get nothing for nothing. / To do nothing is the way to be nothing. / A try is better than nothing. / Fortune favors the brave. / Faint heart never won fair lady. / He who has conquered his own coward spirit has conquered the world. / He who would search for pearls must dive below.

【异】Nothing ventured, nothing have. / Nothing ventured, nothing won.

Chā zhī háo lí, shī zhī qiān lǐ

差之毫厘，失之千里

Voc. 差 fall short of，毫厘 the least bit，失 lose

Lit. An error of the breadth of a single hair can lead a thousand *li* astray.

Exp. It is used to show the importance that people should do things as accurate as possible.

Ex. 甲：翻译的时候，对词义的准确理解很重要。

乙：没错，有个留学生在翻译时，把本意是“张太太和她的先生离婚了，我很同情她”这句话翻译成“张太太和她先生离婚了，我很对不起她”。

甲：真是差之毫厘，失之千里啊。

Quot. 搞科学的人是最严谨的，差之分毫，失之千里嘛。（李良杰《悠悠岁月》）

Cf. 大意失荆州

Var. 失之毫厘，谬以千里/差之分毫，失之千里/差以毫厘，失之千里

A miss is as good as a mile

【义】差一分一毫与差一英里是一样的。

【解】比喻差一点就达到某个目的与完全没有达到结果是相同的。

【例】A：Yesterday at my mother's house I broke a very expensive antique vase by accident.

B：How did that happen?

A：I was taking off my coat and I knocked it down. As it was falling I tried to catch it. I almost caught it. I missed it by an inch but I guess **a miss is as good as a mile.**

B：That's true. It doesn't matter how close you come to catching it. The fact that you narrowly missed catching it is as if you missed catching it by a mile. Anyway, the result is the same: the vase is broken.

【引】He was very near being a poet but a miss is as good as a mile, and he always fell short of the mark. (Sir. Walter Scott, *Journal*, 1825)

【参】Close, but no cigar.

【异】A miff was as good as a smile.

Chī dé kǔ zhōng kǔ, fāng wéi rén shàng rén

吃得苦中苦，方为人上人

Voc. 苦 bitter/hardship，方 only by . . . /can . . . ，为 become

Lit. Only if you can stand the hardest of hardships can you rise in society.

Exp. People get brilliant results primarily because they work hard and take pains rather than they have special inborn powers.

Ex. 甲：你知道吗？小丽要在国家美术馆举办个人画展了。
乙：是吗？她怎么这么厉害？
甲：吃得苦中苦，方为人上人。你不知道她下了多少苦功吗？
乙：她肯定付出了常人难以想象的努力，不然不会有今天的成就。

Quot. 阿杏，年纪轻轻的，怎么想到那上头去呢？吃得苦中苦，方为人上人。你耐心熬着，难道就没个出头之日？（欧阳山《三家巷》）

Cf. 天才出自勤奋/一分耕耘，一分收获/出多少汗，吃多少饭

Var. 受得苦中苦，方为人上人

Genius has an infinite capacity for taking pains

【义】天才就是具有能吃苦的能力。

【解】一个人的才华并不是天生就具有的，而要通过艰苦努力才能获得。

【例】A：Sara is to be an interior designer to decorate the White House.

B：Really! How could she be so wonderful at it?

A：**Genius has an infinite capacity for taking pains**. I know her attention to detail is incredible. She makes notes and draws pictures all the time even when she is on vacation.

B：Exactly. She is meticulous with every detail, and she must have made a great effort to this career. No wonder the government has hired her.

【引】Genius is an infinite capacity for taking pains. But we should still foster it, however much of an embarrassment it may be to us. (M. Bradbury, *Eating People is Wrong*)

【参】Genius is one percent inspiration and ninety-nine percent perspiration.

【异】(Opposite) A genius is born, not made.

Chūtóu de chuánzi xiān làn

出头的椽子先烂

Voc. 出头 jut out，椽子 rafter，烂 rot/worn-out

Lit. Rafters that jut out rot first.

Exp. A person who stands out is liable to get into trouble.

Ex. 甲：你知道马副经理的事吗？
乙：听说他被撤职了。
甲：到底为什么？
乙：听说他在公司大会上讲错了话，一些职工把他告了。
甲：出头的椽子先烂。谁让他这几年升得这么快呢！

Quot. 人常说，出头椽子先烂，你充甚好汉？（马烽《刘胡兰传》）

Cf. 树大招风，官大招险/人怕出名猪怕壮/枪打出头鸟

Var. 出头的鸟遭打，出头的椽先朽/出头椽子先烂，众矢之的（dì）易伤

The post of honor is the post of danger

【义】显赫的职位也是危险的职位。

【解】表示地位越高或名声越大就越容易招人忌妒，引发问题，所以越需要注意。

【例】A：Did you hear about Elaine?

B：I heard she lost her job as the general manager.

A：Really? How come?

B：Some of the employees in her company sued her for being guilty of wrong-doing.

A：Well, I guess **the post of honor is the post of danger**

B：You are right.

【引】The Chancellorship of the Exchequer ... is pre-eminently the post of danger, and therefore the post of honor in the new Government. (*British Weekly*, 1905)

【参】The greater a man's reputation, the greater the criticism. / The highest branch is not the safest roost. / High places have their precipices. / The higher they rise, the steeper they fall.

Dǎ tiě quán kào běnshēn yìng

打铁全靠本身硬

Voc. 打铁 forge iron，靠 depend on，本身 itself，硬 hard

Lit. To forge iron，one must be strong oneself.

Exp. Those who are vulnerable should not attack or educate others. One must be strong and competent to do arduous work.

Ex. 甲：听说许超考上研究生了。

乙：俗话说："打铁全靠本身硬。"许超只有大专文凭，但靠知识改变了命运。

甲：他的进取精神很值得我们学习呀。

Quot. 她才不在乎那一套呢！年轻人就是要经得住摔打，打铁全靠本身硬嘛！（王英先《枫香树》）

Cf. 脚正不怕鞋歪，树正不怕影斜

Var. 打铁先得本身硬，身正影子才不斜/打铁先得锤子硬/打铁贵在硬/打铁要靠本身硬/打铁还须自身硬

Those who live in glass houses shouldn't throw stones

【义】住在玻璃的房子里就不要扔石头。

【解】比喻如果自身是脆弱的或是有弱点的话，就不要去攻击别人。

【例】A：Charlene is so inhospitable, and I dislike staying at her house.

B：Careful what you say.

A：What do you mean?

B：**Those who live in glass houses shouldn't throw stones**. You have not always been pleasant and gracious at your house. For example, you did not even offer me refreshment with dinner. Now, that's like Charlene.

A：I know I have made another mistake. I forgot Charlene is your girlfriend.

【引】People who live in glass houses shouldn't throw stones — and, considering the average U. S. citizens knowledge of world history and geography, we are living in one made of the most fragile glass. (*Newsweek*, 1984)

【参】The pot calling the kettle black. / He who laughs at crooked men should walk very straight.

【异】People who live in glass houses shouldn't throw stones. /Don't throw stones at your neighbors, if your own windows are glass.

Dǎ tiě yào chèn rè, zhì bìng yào chèn zǎo

打铁要趁热，治病要趁早

Voc. 铁 iron，趁 take advantage of (time，opportunity，etc.)，治 cure (an illness)

Lit. Forge iron when it is hot，and treat an illness as soon as it starts.

Exp. Do something immediately when the time is right or/and there is an opportunity. The changes for success are greater if you act at the best possible time.

Ex. 甲：老实说，我想要求老板给我提职加薪。你觉得怎么样？

乙：当然啦。你工作两年多了，我们公司也发展得很快。再说，你最近干得挺出色。

甲：这可难说。我不知道是不是该再等等。我真担心现在提出来老板会不同意。

乙：人们常说："打铁要趁热，治病要趁早。"现在提要求正合适，抓住时机才容易成功。

甲：好，那我就去试试。

Quot. 俗话说："打铁要趁热，治病要趁早。"打官司呢，第一要脑袋尖，才好到处钻营。(吴越《括苍山恩仇记》，第二十七回)

Cf. 机不可失，时不再来/过了这个村，没有这个店/机不可失，时不我待

Var. 趁热打铁/打铁看火候，做事看时机/打铁趁红，做事赶雄

Strike while the iron is hot

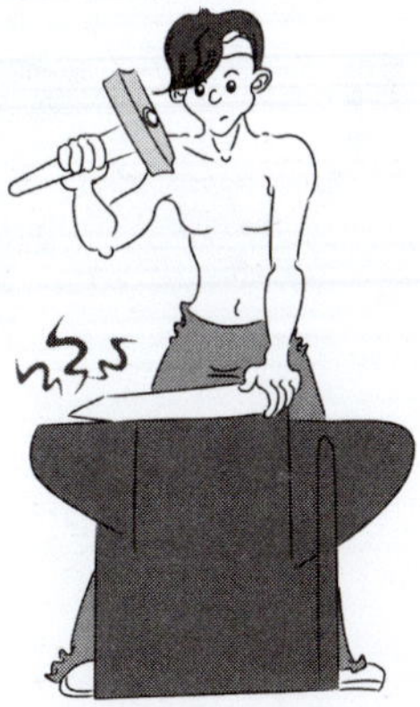

【义】打铁应该趁着它是热的时候。

【解】比喻要抓住最好的时机去做一件事。

【例】A：To be honest, I want to ask the boss for a raise. Do you think it is the time to do that?

B：Of course. You have been working here for more than two years, and our company's growing fast. In addition, you have been doing very well recently.

A：I don't know about that. I wonder if I should wait for a while. I'm afraid of being turned down.

B：Remember that you should **strike while the iron is hot**. It is a good time to make a request. The chance is better if you act at the best possible time.

A：O. K. I guess I'll give it a try.

【引】There was no time to lose. Europe was wide open. Asia too. Now that we had iron, he argued. We should strike while it was hot. (Joseph Hellor, *God Knows*, 1984)

【参】Opportunity seldom knocks twice. / Hoist your sail when the wind is fair. / Make hay while the sun shines. / No time like the present.

【异】You should hammer your iron when it is glowing hot. / Strike while the iron is red.

Dāng duàn bú duàn, bì rě máfan

当断不断，必惹麻烦

Voc. 断 decide，惹 cause，麻烦 trouble

Lit. Indecision when drastic decision is needed breeds trouble.

Exp. It is important to make up one's mind whenever he needs to. Otherwise，nothing can be done，and he will ask for trouble.

Ex. 甲：你拿定主意报考哪所大学了吗？
乙：还没有。这么多学校，不知选哪所好。
甲：报名的截止日期不是快到了吗？
乙：是啊，下星期就停止报名了。
甲：当断不断，必惹麻烦。你迟疑不决，最后恐怕连报名的时间都错过了。

Quot. “天宝，当断不断，必惹麻烦，你是要玉屏，还是要红露和云虹？必须立刻作出抉择。”（周恩惠《珠剑缘》）

Cf. 不怕山高，就怕脚软/疑心生暗鬼，过虑损精神/越怕越摔跤/疑行无成，疑事无功

Var. 当断不断，反受其乱/当断不断，自遭其乱/当断不断，必留后患

He who hesitates is lost

【义】犹豫不定就会失败。(早期主要用于男人对女人的追求)

【解】意指遇事必须拿定主意，坚决果断，才能成功。

【例】A：Donna, how are your college visits? Have you decided on one yet?

B：No, there are so many with biology that I don't know which one to choose.

A：Aren't the deadlines for application fast approaching?

B：I have to give my choice by next week.

A：Remember, **he who hesitates is lost**. If you wait too long, you won't have any choice to make.

B：I know, my grandfather keeps telling me that too. He says that by hesitating or putting this off, I am making a choice not to have a good choice.

【引】"He who hesitates is lost" ... against Martin Hoffman, one of the fastest analysts and players in the game of chess. (*Daily Telegraph*, 1980)

【参】Fortune favors the brave. / Nothing ventured, nothing gained. / Opportunity seldom knocks twice. / Faint heart never won fair lady. / When in doubt, hesitate.

【异】He who hesitates is bossed and usually lost. / He who hesitates is lost. / He who hesitates is sometimes saved.

Dào shénme shān shang chàng shénme gē

到什么山上唱什么歌

Lit. Sing different songs on different mountains.

Exp. Adapt yourself to the customs of the places where you are, and behave as the people around you.

Ex. 甲：对不起，用筷子我什么也夹不起来，还是请服务员给我西餐餐具吧。

乙：别忘了，你现在在中国。到什么山上唱什么歌。要想在中国生活下去，就得学会中国人的生活习惯。学习一些当地人的习俗，你会觉得你的旅行更有意思。

甲：我同意。但是，如果现在没有叉子的话，我恐怕只能用手吃饭了。

Quot. 俗话说："到什么山上唱什么歌儿"，又说："看菜吃饭，量体裁衣"。我们无论做什么事都要看情况办理。（毛泽东《反对党八股》）

Cf. 入乡随俗，骑马随鞍/到哪河，脱哪鞋/到什么山上打什么柴/到什么山上砍什么柴/进什么林，打什么鸟

Var. 到哪座山唱哪个歌/到哪山，唱哪歌/到哪山头唱哪歌/到哪架山梁，唱哪架山歌

When in Rome, do as the Romans do

【义】在罗马的时候就要像罗马人那样做。

【解】比喻不管到什么地方，都要按照当地人的习惯去做。

【例】A：Chopsticks! I can never pick up a piece of meat with them. I had better ask the waitress to give me a spoon or a fork. Hi, excuse me . . .

B：Hey, you are in China now. Remember that **when in Rome, do as the Romans do**. To make yourself feel at home, I think, this is one of the things that you have to learn. I always tell myself to follow the customs of the local people when traveling. You may enjoy your trip more if you can pick up some local customs.

A：Well, I agree. However, I would have to use my hands to eat without a fork.

【引】"I thought the English never bothered about protocol!" "When in Rome, however, we do as the Romans do." (N. Mitford, *Don't tell Alfred viii.*, 1960)

To raise money in America, do as the Americans do. (*New York Times*, 1992)

【参】A man's home is his castle. / New lords, new laws. / Stretch your arm no further than your sleeve will reach.

【异】When you are at Rome do as they do there. / Do at Rome as the Romans do. / When in Rome, do as Rome does.

Gǎn shíwǔ bùrú gǎn chūyī

赶十五不如赶初一

Voc. 赶 try to catch, 不如 not as good as, 初一 the first day of the lunar month

Lit. try to catch the beginning of the month rather than the middle

Exp. Do what you are supposed to do as early as you can. / Don't delay things you should do.

Ex. 甲：你做完功课了吗？
乙：没有，我还没有开始做呢。
甲：为什么？你现在就应该做。
乙：急什么？反正下个星期才交呢。
甲：赶十五不如赶初一。别拖来拖去，火烧眉毛才着急。
乙：好吧。我也听说拖拉是时间的小偷，该做的事最好早点儿做。

Quot. 分田是天大的好事，赶十五不如赶初一，好事要越快办越好。（吴南生《革命母亲李梨英》）

Cf. 明日复明日，明日何其多/时间好像东流水，只能流去不流回/没有时时刻刻，就没有年年月月

Var. 赶早不赶晚/赶前不赶后/赶早不赶晚，宜早不宜迟

Don't put off till tomorrow what should be done today

【义】你今天能做的事就不要等到明天。

【解】做事情不应该毫无必要地拖延。

【例】A: Have you finished your homework assignment yet?

B: No. I haven't even started it.

A: Why not? You should do it now.

B: What's the hurry? It isn't even due until next week anyway.

A: **Don't put off till tomorrow what should be done today.** If you procrastinate, you may have to hurry in the end or you may never finish at all.

B: You're right. It's said that procrastination is the thief of time. It is best to finish things early.

【引】Good executives never put off until tomorrow what they can get someone else to do today. (*Bits & Pieces*, 1987)

【异】(Opposite) Always put off till tomorrow what needs to be done today. / Never do today what you can put off till tomorrow.

Gēbo nǐng bu guò dàtuǐ

胳膊拧不过大腿

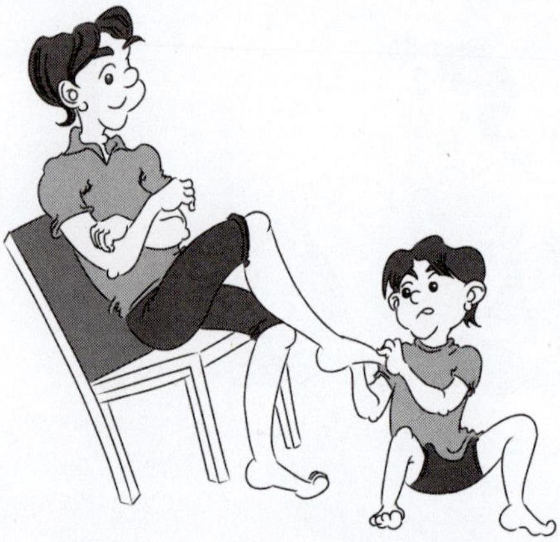

Voc. 胳膊 arm，大腿 thigh，拧 twist

Lit. The arm is no match for the thigh.

Exp. It's wise to give up if you realize there's no hope to defeat your opponent.

Ex. 甲：真倒霉，紧挨着我们家小吃店的那家新饭店下星期就开张了。听说老板是个大富翁，他们还请了本城最好的经理和厨师。我们怎么能跟他们竞争啊？

乙：依我看，胳膊拧不过大腿，鸡蛋碰不过石头。如果你竞争不过，还不如跟他们合作，或者给他们干活儿。

甲：对，明天我就去找他们的老板谈谈。

Quot. 刘冬生摆摆手，劝道："大伯，使不得、使不得，鸡蛋碰不过石头，胳膊拧不过大腿，还是避开为上策。"（武剑青《云飞峰》）

Cf. 鸡蛋碰不过石头/小鬼斗不过阎王/识时务者为俊杰/好汉不吃眼前亏/猫不与狗斗，穷不跟富斗

Var. 胳膊扭不过大腿

If you can't beat them, join them

【义】如果你不能打败他们的话，就加入到他们之中。

【解】表示要认清时务。如果你不能击败你的竞争对手，不如加入到他们之中，跟他们一起做。

【例】A：What a bad luck! The new restaurant next to our family snack bar is going to open its business next week. It was said that they have hired the best manager and cooks in town, and the owner is a millionaire. How can we compete with them?

B：Well, I understand that it is going to be a difficult situation for you. However, **if you can't beat them, join them**.

A：That is right. My parents also told me that if I can't defeat my opponents, join forces with them. My business might get better by joining the new restaurant. I'll talk to the owner tomorrow.

【引】I said, running things, what's the point? He said, if you can't beat them, join them! (D. Lessing, *Shikasta 266*, 1979)

Roy Vagelos, CEO of the undisputed champ of the pharmaceutical industry, concluded: If you can't beat 'em, buy 'em. (*Fortune*, 1993)

【参】Self-preservation is the first law of nature.

【异】If you can't lick 'em, join 'em. / If you can't beat 'em, starve 'em. / If you can't lick 'em, buy 'em. / If you can't kill them, join 'em. / If you can't fight 'em, debate 'em.

Gōngfu bú fù yǒuxīnrén

功夫不负有心人

Voc. 功夫 effort，负 let down，有心人 a person with high aspirations and determination

Lit. Those who work hard will be rewarded.

Exp. Your goal won't be achieved without hard work and determination.

Ex. 甲：哎哟，真受不了这样的训练，我全身又酸又疼。

乙：我知道。新来的这位足球教练严极了，我从小到大没跑过这么长的路。

甲：你难道忘了教练总是说，"功夫不负有心人"嘛！

乙：是啊。我也知道他是对的。如果不费力气就能成功，那么人人都成功了。现在吃苦才能有将来的成绩。

Quot. 功夫不负有心人。聂卫平在训练班里学艺一年，棋艺大有长进。（朱小明《棋坛旋风聂卫平》）

Cf. 一分耕耘，一分收获/出多少汗，吃多少饭/三分天才，七分勤劳/人勤地听话，志坚石结瓜/樱桃好吃树难栽，不下苦功花不开

Var. 功夫不亏有心人/功夫不废有心人/功夫不负苦心人/功夫不亏用心人

No pains, no gains

【义】pain 痛苦，gain 收获。没有痛苦就没有收获。

【解】不能吃苦就得不到你所需要的。常用于体育运动。

【例】A：Wow！What a tough practice，I'm really tired and my muscles are sore.

B：I know. That new soccer coach is really tough. I never ran so much in my life.

A：Still，you know what the coach always says：**No pains，no gains**.

B：Yes，I suppose he's correct，too. If success required no hardship，everyone would be successful. It's necessary to sacrifice comfort now for a success in the future.

【引】Now，remember，people，no pains，no gains！I want you out on the volleyball court in full sweats every day at 9：00！（A. B. Trudeau，*Doonesbury Deluxe*，1989）

【参】No sweat，no sweet. / Nothing ventured，nothing gained. / You can't make an omelette without breaking eggs.

【异】There are no gains without pains. / Pain past is pleasure. / What pains us trains us. / Nothing comes without pain except dirty and long nails.

Gū zhù yí zhì, bú shì quán yíng, jiù shì quán shū

孤注一掷，不是全赢，就是全输

Voc. 孤 single，注 bet (in gambling)，掷 throw，赢 win，输 lose

Lit. risk everything on a single throw / bet one's last dollar

Exp. Don't risk everything in a single undertaking.

Ex. 甲：你的中文课怎么样？

乙：我的成绩不好，而且常常不去上课。

甲：为什么？

乙：我在准备考 HSK。只要考得好，中文课得什么成绩都没关系。

甲：孤注一掷，不是全赢，就是全输。平时成绩很重要，而且上课能帮助你考好 HSK。再说，要是你考不好呢？

Quot. “款子没还有汇来，可是我们要放手干一干。”“哦，那么老赵也是孤注一掷了……”（茅盾《子夜》）

Cf. （反）狡兔必有三窟

Don't put all your eggs in one basket

【义】别把你所有的鸡蛋都放在一个篮子里。

【解】比喻不要投入全部的力量、财产等去冒险做某一件事。

【例】A：How is your English class going?

B：Well, I haven't done so well in my quizzes and I've missed several classes as well. We have a big composition for our final project on which I'm planning to do a really good job. That should impress the teacher and save my grade too.

A：**Don't put all your eggs in one basket**. If you have an accident, you might break them all. You shouldn't count on your final project to save your grade. What if you don't do as well on it as you expect? Your grade will suffer because you've only focused on one thing.

【引】A wise man once said, "If you put all your eggs in one basket, watch that basket." When it comes to stocks, if you put all your eggs in one basket, watch out. (*Wall Street Journal*, 1991)

【参】The mouse that has but one hole is quickly taken.

【异】Don't carry all your eggs in one basket. / One can't afford to put all one's eggs in one basket.

Guāngtóu yuándǐng de bù yídìng dōu shì héshang

光头圆顶的不一定都是和尚

Voc. 光头圆顶 bare head，和尚 monk

Lit. All that bares his head is not a monk.

Exp. The appearance of a thing or a person could be deceptive. Nothing should be judged by its appearance.

Ex. 甲：祝贺你！毕业了，一定很激动吧？

乙：说真的，并不完全像想象中那样。俗话说，光头圆顶的不一定都是和尚。戴上了学士帽，心里却感到不踏实，还得好好修炼才行。

甲：是啊。学位肯定是来之不易的，要做到名副其实就更不容易了。

Quot. 光头光脑不都是和尚，发光闪亮不定是黄金。（贵州省集成谚语卷《侗族谚语》）

Cf. 才人无貌，烂扇子多风/人不可貌相，海水不可斗量/好马不在铃铛响/好茶不在颜色浓/名山不在高

Var. 光头光脑不都是和尚

All that glitters is not gold

【义】闪闪发光的不一定都是金子。

【解】看起来光亮耀眼的东西并不一定都是货真价实。常用于提醒或警告。

【例】A: Carl, congratulations on your graduation! You must be extremely excited.

B: Well, to tell you the truth, the graduation isn't all it seems to be. **All that glitters is not gold**, I guess. I don't think I have learned enough.

A: That's true. The degree certainly comes at a high price. However, because a stone that is shiny and glittery does not mean it is gold, so too the things that sometimes sound or look so attractive are really not so attractive once they're attained.

【引】... after getting those purchased home, you soon realize that all that glitters is not gold. (*Reader's Digest*, 1991)

【参】Don't judge a book by its cover. / Appearances are deceiving. / Never judge by appearances.

【异】All is not gilt that glitters. / All is not gold that glitters.

Guòle hé jiù chāi qiáo, bù liú hòu lù

过了河就拆桥，不留后路

Voc. 过 pass，拆 take down，桥 bridge

Lit. take down one's bridge after passing it

Exp. hurt or cause pain to someone that has helped in solving the problems

Ex. 甲：小张，请你以后不要再给我打电话了。

乙：什么？刚帮你找到房子，就不认老朋友啦？

甲：租房子我自己付房租，也不欠你什么。我觉得，咱们性格不同，没必要再交往了。

乙：不要过了河就拆桥，不留后路。别忘了，你以后还有要"过河"的时候。

Quot. 平儿咬牙道："没良心的东西，过了河就拆桥。"（《红楼梦》，第二十一回）

Cf. 鸟尽弓藏，兔死狗烹/卸完磨就杀驴

Var. 过桥抽板，上屋抽梯

Don't bite the hand that feeds you

【义】别咬喂你东西吃的手。

【解】告诫你一个人不要去伤害那些帮助或照顾过自己的人。

【例】A：Why do you always argue with your mom? You even don't want to talk to her. It seems that you make her very sad and disappointed.

B：You don't understand, Grandpa. There is a big generation gap. She always feels that I must listen to her for everything. Actually, I'm not a child any more!

A：Well, have you seen how hard your mom has been working in order to pay for your college education? All she wants is to see your success. **Don't bite the hand that feeds you**. My suggestion is you shouldn't hurt someone who takes care of you.

【引】"Hasn't anyone ever told you 'Don't bite the hand that feeds you'? You must know how disappointed I am!" "I'm sorry, Dad. I don't mean to hurt you after all you've done for me." (H. Collis, *101 American English Proverbs*, 1992)

Mr. Bush said the Democrat-controlled Congress had blocked his package to spur economic growth. "I extended my hand to the Democratic leaders, and they bit it," he said. (*New York Times*, 1992)

【异】Don't bite the hand that butter you bread.

Guòle zhège cūn, méiyǒu zhège diàn

过了这个村，没有这个店

Voc. 村 village，店 store

Lit. There won't be a store like this after passing this village.

Exp. If you have an opportunity to do something, do it before the opportunity passes.

Ex. 甲：你跟我们一起去工作招聘会吗？我听说电话公司要招人。

乙：真的？我喜欢这种工作，而且我觉得我一定够条件。但是，我这个星期想跟我的朋友去度假，下次再说吧。

甲：别傻了。过了这个村，没有这个店。像这样的工作，不是你什么时候要就什么时候有的。

乙：那我们的假期计划呢？我朋友会失望的。

甲：把你的想法告诉他就行了。做事得抓住有利时机，度假可以以后再说。

Quot. 该快活的时候还不敢去干，地道的傻子；过了这村便没有这店。（老舍《骆驼祥子》）

Cf. 机不可失，时不再来/过了此山无此鸟/见物不取，失之千里

Var. 过了这村儿，没有这店儿

Make hay while the sun shines

【义】趁有太阳翻晒干草。

【解】做事要抓住有利时机，不要错过。

【例】A：Do you want to come with us to the job fair? I heard that the telephone company is looking for operators.

B：Really! I like that kind of job, and I think I am qualified for it. However, I'm planning a vacation with my friend. Maybe I will give it a try next time.

A：Come on, don't make a fool of yourself. You should **make hay while the sun shines**. Job opportunities like this don't come around often.

B：Well, what about my vacation, then? My friend will be disappointed.

A：Just tell him that you should take advantage of an opportunity to do something when it is available, and take a vacation with him sometime later.

【引】As long as you are unemployed, you might as well use your spare time to clean the house thoroughly. Make hay while the sun shines. (Anne Bertram, *NTC's Dictionary of Proverbs and Clichés*, 1993)

【参】Strike while the iron is hot. / Take the goods the gods provide. / Time and tide wait for no man. / No time like the present. / Opportunity never knocks twice. / Every dog has his day. / The mill cannot grind with the water that is past.

【异】When the sun shines make hay.

Hǎo de kāishǐ jiù shì chénggōng de yíbàn
好的开始就是成功的一半

Voc. 开始 beginning，成功 success，半 half

Lit. A good beginning is half of a success.

Exp. Any endeavor with a good foundation is likely to succeed.

Ex. 甲：今天真痛快，特别是早上，我们的新商店刚一开张就来了那么多顾客。

乙：这只是第一天，以后的生意还不知道怎么样呢。

甲：别忘了，好的开始就是成功的一半。

乙：既然我们已经成功一半了，那么希望今后也一定没有问题。

Cf. 万事开头难/头三脚难踢/头三脚难踢，开锣的戏难唱/万事从一开始/善始必善终

A good beginning is half the battle

【义】好的开始就是胜利的保证。

【解】比喻凡事第一步很重要。有个好的开始就会为今后的成功打下基础。

【例】A：What a great day，especially this morning. We were able to get all the corn planted.

B：And tonight we can celebrate with singing and dancing.

A：You know **a good beginning is half the battle**.

B：I think it is true. Our morning work is finished，and this evening we can rest and celebrate with others.

A：What a good day!

【引】"The single market is only half the battle without a single currency，" said Keith Richardson，the secretary general of the European Roundtable. （*New York Times*，1993）

【参】A good beginning makes a good ending. / The first blow is half the battle. / The first step is the hardest. / Good seed makes a good crop.

【异】A good beginning is half done.

Hǎoshì bù chū mén, èshì chuán qiān lǐ

好事不出门，恶事传千里

Voc. 恶事 bad news，传 spread，千里 a thousand *li*

Lit. Good news never goes beyond the gate, while bad news spreads a thousand *li* away.

Exp. Stay away from bad things or problems, since bad news spreads far away, much further than good news.

Ex. 甲：听说你昨天旷课了，为什么？

乙：你怎么知道的？

甲：好事不出门，恶事传千里。你的同学早就告诉我了。

乙：昨天我为了查找资料，自己在图书馆看了一天书，我刻苦用功怎么没人向你报告！

Quot. 好事不出门，恶事传千里，他们这个好笑的话柄，一人传十，十人传百，又经过了多嘴多舌的人添油加醋，竟把菊咬金涂成了花鼻子了。(周立波《山乡巨变》)

Cf. 要想人不知，除非己莫为/人有名，树有影/宁可折骨头，不可败名声

Var. 好事不出门，丑事传千里/好事不出名，坏事一溜风/好事不出门，坏事传天下

Bad news travels fast

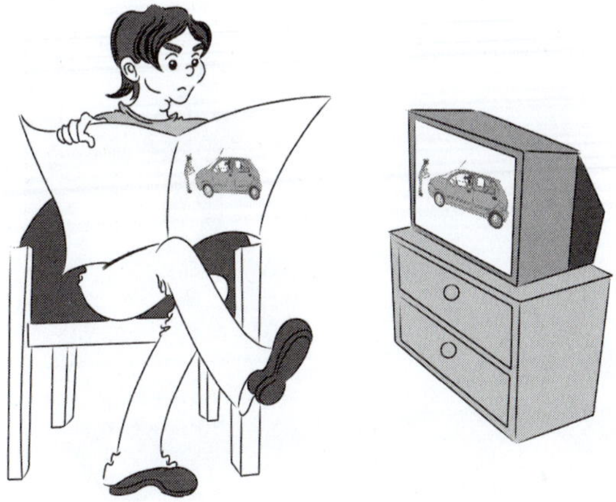

【义】坏消息传得快。

【解】告诫人们要努力把事情做好，尽量避免出现问题，因为坏事很容易传开。

【例】A：Hi！I'm sorry to hear you got fired.

B：How did you know about that already? It only happened this morning.

A：**Bad news travels fast**.

B：I hope I can find a new job soon.

A：Good luck. However, good news travels slowly.

【引】Bad news travels fast. Good news takes the scenic route. （*Cartoon by Doug Larson*, 1990）

【参】No news is good news. / A bad thing never dies.

【异】Ill news travels fast. / Bad news travels like lightning. / Good news travels slowly; bad news travels fast. / Bad news has wings. / Bad news always comes too soon.

Hǎo xiōngdì gāo dǎ qiáng, qīnqi péngyou yuǎn lí xiāng

好兄弟高打墙，亲戚朋友远离乡

Voc. 兄弟 brothers，打墙 build a wall，亲戚 relative，离乡 be away from home

Lit. Good brothers build tall walls between them, and relatives and friends are away from their hometown.

Exp. It suggests that it is better to keep a certain distance between relatives and friends if they want to maintain a good relationship.

Ex. 甲：你看，我们的邻居请客，结果他朋友的车都停到我们家门口了。

乙：是啊，连门都出不去，怎么办？

甲：给邻居打电话，让他的朋友把车都开走。

乙：这样他会生气吧？

甲：好兄弟高打墙，亲戚朋友远离乡。虽然是街坊邻居，也得分清界线，这样才不会互相干扰。

Quot. “他们相好虽相好，”农会说，“可不愿搅在一块。正月里善人就有这个意思，试探行政，行政说，好兄弟高打墙，亲戚朋友远离乡。……”（柳青《种谷记》）

Cf. 亲兄弟，明算账/亲戚门外客/亲是亲，财是财

Good fences make good neighbors

【义】有好围墙才有好邻居。

【解】表示邻居之间应该保持距离，尊重对方，这样才不至于互相干扰，有利于保持良好的关系。

【例】A：Kyle is letting his friends park on part of our yard for his picnic today.

B：I see there are several cars along the edge.

A：What are we going to do?

B：Well, **good fences make good neighbors**.

A：I wish he would be more respectful and ask our permission before he lets his friends park on the lawn. Neighbors should respect one another and pay attention to other people's interest.

【引】My apple trees will never get across and eat the cones under his pines, I tell him. He only says, "Good fences make good neighbors." (R. Frost, *North of Boston*)

While its advocates cited the phrase that "good fences make good neighbors," in the area of national security what is far more true is that "good neighbors make good friends." (*Manhattan Jewish Sentinel*, 1995)

【参】A hedge between keeps friendship green. / An Englishman's house is his castle. / Familiarity breeds contempt.

【异】Love your neighbor, yet pull not down your fence.

Hòuhuǐyào méi chù mǎi

后悔药没处买

Voc. 后悔 regret，药 medicine，处 place

Lit. There is no place to purchase the medicine for remorse.

Exp. Don't grieve or regret about having done something that can't be undone.

Ex. 甲：真糟糕！昨天是我姐姐的生日，可是我忘了。
乙：我相信你姐姐会原谅你的。她知道你在学校非常忙。
甲：但愿如此。但是我至少应该给她打个电话。
乙：算了，后悔药没处买。这个周末你可以去看她，说不定给她一个惊喜呢。

Quot. 人们常说，后悔药没处买，此时，白广利正应了这句话。（董玉振《精明人的苦恼》）

Cf. 泼出的水收不回/覆水难收/好马不吃回头草/开弓没有回头箭/泼水难收/泼出的水，收不回；咽下的米，吐不出/泼出去的水，嫁出去的女

Var. 后悔药吃了没用/后悔药没处寻/千金难买后悔药

Don't cry over spilt milk

【义】别对着已经洒了的牛奶哭。

【解】比喻不要为已经发生或做过而又不能挽回的事情悲伤或苦恼。

【例】A: I feel bad. Yesterday was my sister's birthday, but I forgot.

B: I'm sure your sister will forgive you. She knows you are very busy with school.

A: I hope so. It is the end of the school year, but I should have at least called her.

B: Well, **don't cry over spilt milk**. You can probably show up this weekend to give her a big surprise.

【引】It's no use crying over spilt milk. The money's gone and that's that. (M. De La Roche, *Whiteoak Harvest xxv*, 1936)

Looking back, I should have pursued philosophy and history and economics and things of that sort in college more, but I didn't. But I am not going to cry over spilt milk and that's past me. (Quayle, *New York Times Magazine*, 1986)

【参】What's done cannot be undone. / What's done is done. / Things past cannot be recalled. / It is too late to shut the stable door after the horse has bolted. / A broken egg can't be put back together.

【异】It is no use crying over spilt milk.

Huā yán qiǎo yǔ bú jì shì

花言巧语不济事

Voc. 花言 sweet words，巧语 fine words，不济事 of no use

Lit. Sweet words and fine words are not of any help.

Exp. Nothing is ever achieved by fine words alone. Just because someone promises something does not guarantee that he or she will do it. It can be used as a rebuke, implying that the person who is promising something will not do it.

Ex. 甲：我的男朋友说我们结婚以后就给我买辆新汽车。
乙：你还相信他！难道你忘了他常常不守信用吗？
甲：我想他这次是真的。
乙：别忘了，花言巧语不济事。
甲：是呀，以前他常常是说得好听，说完了就算了。
乙：那你这次为什么还要相信他？

Quot. 现在轮到你们这些人用花言巧语来欺骗青年了。（巴金《给山川均先生》）

Cf. 花木瓜，空好看/说一千，道一万，二横一竖就靠干/好话不能当饭吃/大话好听不抵债/万句言语吃不饱，一捧流水能解渴/一千个嘴把式，不如一个真把式/嘴皮上不会长庄稼

Fine words butter no parsnips

【义】好听的话不能当黄油用。(parsnips，一种蔬菜，根部可食用。西方人习惯在上面涂抹黄油。)

【解】比喻光靠说做不成事，不能相信一个人怎么说，要看他怎么做。可用来斥责一个人不守信用，答应的事却不去做。

【例】A：Tom is going to buy me a new car after we are married.

B：Do you believe him after all the other promises he failed to keep?

A：He is not like that now.

B：**Fine words butter no parsnips**.

A：Well, I know he has said things, and made many promises and then broken them in the past.

B：He certainly has, and I don't know why you'd believe him now.

【引】Fine words butter no parsnips. Who will help me to reopen my shop? Who will build me a house? (M. Westmacott, *Rose & Yew Tree*)

【参】Deeds, not words. / He who gives fair words feeds you with an empty spoon. / Praise without profit puts little in the pot. / The greatest talkers are the least doers.

Huà shé tiān zú, nòng qiǎo chéng zhuō

画蛇添足，弄巧成拙

Voc. 蛇 snake，添 add，足 foot，巧 clever，拙 blunder

Lit. draw a snake and add feet to it

Exp. try to change what is already adequate

Ex. 甲：小丽，你的发型有点儿奇怪。是不是理发师给你理坏了？

乙：别提了，我昨天理完发后，觉得不太理想，就自己对着镜子修理了一下。没想到，不小心剪多了，结果成了这个样子。

甲：咳，这可真是“画蛇添足，弄巧成拙”。我再帮你修补一下吧。

乙：什么？你还要再画蛇添足吗？

Quot. 将军功绩已成，威声大震，可以止矣。今若前进，倘不如意，正如画蛇添足也。（《三国演义》，第一一零回）

Cf. 画蛇添足，多此一举/画蛇添足，徒劳无功

Var. 画蛇添脚，弄巧成拙

Leave well enough alone

【义】不要去改变已经做好的事或东西。

【解】比喻如果做事多此一举，反而会弄巧成拙。

【例】A：Hey，where's Rita?

B：She's still in hospital，her doctor won't let her leave the hospital for another day.

A：Oh no！I thought she was able to go out with us this evening.

B：She would have been able to，but when her doctor asked her if she was ready to go home，Rita answered that she wanted to take more medicine before leaving the hospital. As a result，she was sick again due to overtaking the drug. She should learn to **leave well enough alone**. She certainly didn't help the situation by causing more aggravation. Sometimes it's just best to leave things as they are.

【引】Scarlett hold her peace，for it was easier to let well enough alone，and life went on smoothly enough，on the surface.（Margaret Mitchell，*Gone with the Wind*，1936）

Tall said no more，and so neither did Stein. He was willing enough to let well enough alone.（James Jones，*The Thin Red Line*，1962）

【参】Go farther and fare worse. / Enough is as good as a feast. / Let sleeping dogs sleep. / If it isn't broke，don't fix it. / He who would be too clever makes a fool of himself.

【异】Let well enough alone. / Let well or ill alone. / Leave bad enough alone. / Better let well enough alone.

Huànnàn jiàn zhìjiāo

患难见至交

Voc. 患难 adversity，至交 best friend

Lit. A best friend is found in adversity.

Exp. It's easy to see who are real friends in time of need or hardship.

Ex. 甲：听说你的公司生意很红火。
乙：还可以。
甲：前一阵是不是遇上些麻烦？
乙：是啊。一些人当时就离我而去了，只有几个好朋友留了下来，一起坚持让公司挺过来了。
甲：真是患难见至交啊！

Quot. 患难见至交，烈火现真金。在关键的时候，最能看出一个人的高贵品质。（峻青《雄关赋 · 乡情》）

Cf. 患难朋友，艰苦夫妻/岁寒知松柏，患难见人心/雪中送炭真君子，锦上添花是小人/疾风识劲草，患难见真情

Var. 患难见人心/患难结知己/患难见朋友/患难识忠臣

A friend in need is a friend indeed

【义】在需要时出现的朋友才是真正的朋友。

【解】真正的友谊往往在患难之中才能体现出来。

【例】A：I am glad you stopped. My car has broken down and there is no phone for miles.

B：It was not a problem. I've been in your situation before, and someone stopped to help me.

A：**A friend in need is a friend indeed**

B：Exactly, when someone needs assistance, it is a true friend that stops to help.

【引】Our great "friend" in Washington is shooting out wildly in our direction, proving in effect that "a friend in need is a friend indeed," as long as it is his need. (*New York Times*, 1986)

【参】Prosperity makes friends and adversity tries them.

Huó dào lǎo, xué dào lǎo

活到老，学到老

Voc. 活 live，老 old

Lit. learn as long as one lives

Exp. Never stop learning in your lifetime, since there are always some things that one can learn at any age.

Ex. 甲：你爷爷身体怎么样？最近在做什么？
乙：他今年81了，身体特别好。他正打算上一个“老年大学”。
甲：真的？在“老年大学”学习什么呀？
乙：听说他们要学太极拳。
甲：你爷爷以前打过太极拳吗？
乙：没有。但是他常对我说，“活到老，学到老”。他总是喜欢学新的东西，这恐怕是他看起来不显老的原因吧？
甲：可不是嘛！一个人上了年纪并不意味着他就得放弃学习。

Quot. 大哥，这是为国家干活，还怕为多学习低低头吗？你不是常说，人要活到老，学到老吗？（老舍《青年突击队》）

Cf. 人老不算老，心老才算老/活着一辈子，学着一辈子/活到九十九，书本不离手/知识无底，学海无边/读不尽的书，走不完的路/海水舀不完，知识学不完

Var. 活到老，学到老，九十九岁学个巧/活到老，学到老，还有三件没学到

One is never too old to learn

【义】你永远不会因为年纪大而不能学习。

【解】一个人在任何时候都可以学习。

【例】A: Hey, how is your grandfather doing these days?

B: Great! He just had his 81st birthday and his health is perfect. In fact he is thinking of taking an exercise class for senior citizens.

A: Wow, that's really something. What types of things will they be doing in the exercise class?

B: I heard they are going to learn shadow boxing.

A: Has your grandfather ever done shadow boxing before?

B: No, but he always tells me, "**One is never too old to learn.**" He always likes to learn new things. I think that's why he seems so young.

A: That's really great. Just because a person is old does not mean they have to stop learning things.

【引】Leaning is a lifelong process. It's never too late to learn what you need to succeed. (*Wall Street Journal's National Business Employment Weekly*, 1991)

【参】Live and learn. / It's never too late to mend.

【异】It's never too late to learn.

Jiā hé quán kào rénxīn hé

家和全靠人心和

Voc. 和 harmonious, 靠 depend on, 人心 popular feeling

Lit. If the family lives in harmony, it depends on the will of the family members.

Exp. Only if every family member shares the same will and feeling, a family can stay together harmoniously.

Ex. 甲：新上任的领导班子怎么样？

乙：看起来很团结。

甲：家和全靠人心和。作为企业，首先要领导班子和。

乙：对，看来咱们公司的发展指日可待了。

Quot. 家和全靠人心和。一个家庭的和睦，全靠全家人的心齐。（王卿、刘书祥《谚语小辞典》）

Cf. 家和万事兴/人和万事兴/家有一心，有钱买金；家有二心，无钱买针/弟兄三人三条心，万贯家财不够分；弟兄三人一条心，黄土也能变成金/人和天地顺，家和万事兴

The family that prays together stays together

【义】在一起祈祷的家庭成员能够生活在一起。

【解】只有想法和目标一致，家庭成员才能团结，和睦相处。

【例】A：I have to go and meet my family for church before we go to the basketball game.

B：Boy, your family sure spends a lot of time together. Doesn't it get annoying always being around your family?

A：No, we enjoy spending time together because everyone is so precious; church is an important part of our life.

B：I guess **the family that prays together stays together**.

A：Yes, I would agree with that. Prayer helps us work out any of our family problems and it binds us together.

【引】"More things are wrought by prayer than this world dreams of", and "the family that prays together stays together". (*St. Joseph Magazine*, 1948)

Jiāngshān yì gǎi, běnxìng nán yí

江山易改，本性难移

Voc. 江山 land，改 change，本性 natural instinct，移 remove

Lit. It's easy to change rivers and mountains but hard to change a person's nature.

Exp. Lifelong habits or inherited characteristics can't be concealed. It is often used in a derogatory sense.

Ex. 甲：听说小五又被抓起来送回监狱了。

乙：他从小就跟流氓混在一起，他的父母也从来不管他。他上个月刚一放出来就找他的那帮哥们儿去了，连家也没回。

甲：难怪！真是江山易改，本性难移。

Quot. 真是江山易改，本性难移。这个苏女生总喜欢咋咋呼呼，虚张声势。（戴厚英《人啊，人》）

Cf. 是狗就会吃屎，是狼改不了吃肉/狗嘴里吐不出象牙/一缸不出两样酒，一树不开两样花/蛇入竹筒，曲性难改/乌鸦插上羽毛也变不成凤凰/坏笋生不了好竹子

Var. 江山易改，秉性难移/江山好改，秉性难移/山河易改，本性难移

What is bred in the bone will never come out of the flesh

【义】生在骨头里的东西永远不会从身上出来。

【解】生下来就带有的本性不会改变。

【例】A：Do you know Tom has been arrested and put back in prison?

B：I heard about that. He has been hanging around with gang members ever since he was a child, and his parents have never paid enough attention to his problem.

A：No wonder. **What is bred in the bone will never come out of the flesh**.

【引】We will always be farmers, for what is bred in the bone will never come out in the flesh. (L. I. Wilder, *First Four Years*, 1991)

【参】Blood will tell. / An ape's an ape, a varlet's a varlet. / Boys will be boys. / The child is the father to the man. / What can you expect from a pig but a grunt? / Once a thief, always a thief. / The leopard does not change his spots. / He who fights and runs away, may live to fight another day.

【异】What's bred in the bone will out. / What is bred in the bone will never out of the flesh. / What is bred in the bone will tell. / What's bred in the bone can't be beaten out with a stick. / What's bred in the bone stays there.

Jìn zhū zhě chì, jìn mò zhě hēi

近朱者赤，近墨者黑

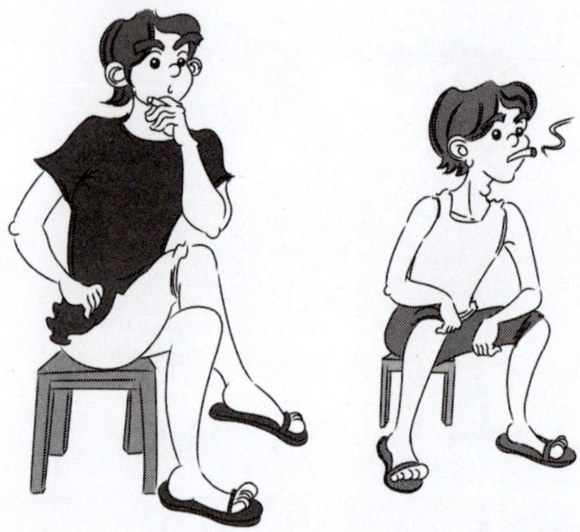

Voc. 朱 cinnabar，赤 red，墨 ink，黑 black

Lit. One who nears cinnabar becomes red and one who nears ink becomes black.

Exp. Your personalities, character or reputation will be greatly influenced by association, so choose your friends carefully.

Ex. 甲：汤姆，我觉得奇怪，你为什么常和那些赌博的人搞在一起？

乙：那又怎么样？我们互相认识很久了，反正我又不赌博。

甲：你知道吗？跟谁交往得小心。近朱者赤，近墨者黑。

乙：难道人们会相信，一个人的朋友是什么样，他就是什么样？

甲：可不是嘛！

Quot. “常言道：‘近朱者赤，近墨者黑。’那怪在此，断知水性。我们如今拿住他，且不要打杀，只叫他送师父过河。”（吴承恩《西游记》）

Cf. 欲知其人，视其朋友，当观其偶/挨着铁匠会打铁，挨着木匠会拉锯

Var. 近鲍者臭，近兰者香/挨金似金，挨玉似玉

A man is known by the company he keeps

【义】从其交友知其为人。

【解】告诫人们要注意选择朋友。因为物以类聚，人以群分。

【例】A：Tom, I wonder why you are hanging around with those people.

B：So what? We have known each other for a long time, and I am not a criminal anyway.

A：Look, you have to be careful about who you associate with. **A man is known by the company he keeps**.

B：Is that true people believe that a person is like his friends?

A：Unfortunately, yes.

【引】You can tell a lobbyist in Washington by the company that keeps him. (*Wall Street Journal*, 1992)

【参】Birds of a feather flock together. /As a man is, so is his company. / Tell me what company you keep, and I'll tell you what you are. (Spanish) /If you lie down with dogs, you will get up with fleas. /He who goes with wolves learns to howl.

【异】A man is judged by the company he keeps. /A man is known by the friends he knows. / A man is known by the company he keeps, and a woman is known by the company she is kept by.

Lǎohǔ hái yǒu dǎdǔnr de shíhou

老虎还有打盹儿的时候

Voc. 老虎 tiger，打盹儿 nod

Lit. Even a tiger will nod sometimes.

Exp. Nobody can be at his best all the time. Even the best of us are liable to make mistakes.

Ex. 甲：你是不是累了？

乙：是有点儿。平时我好像从来不知道什么叫累，浑身总有使不完的劲儿。可是今天是觉得有点儿没精神了。

甲：老虎还有打盹儿的时候。你虽然年轻，但也得注意劳逸结合。

Quot. 人有失手，马有漏蹄，老虎还有打盹儿时候，只要咱们不死，机会总会有的。（单田芳《燕王剑侠》）

Cf. 智者千虑，必有一失/人有失手，马有失蹄/人非圣贤，谁能无过

Var. 老虎也有打瞌睡的时候

Homer sometimes nods

【义】荷马（古希腊诗人）也有打盹儿的时候。

【解】表示任何人都难免有疏忽的时候。

【例】A：Sam, you are tired.

B：I am. But the strange thing is that I am never tired. Normally, I feel like I have tons of energy, but today I have none.

A：Well, even **Homer sometimes nods**

B：What?

A：I mean that everyone, even you, needs a break in order to rest and let their minds and bodies sleep.

【引】"I've done that trip twenty times or more. I know every inch of the road ... but today I took a wrong turning and lost myself." "Those things do happen. Even Homer sometimes nods." (R. Ridout & C. Witting, *English Proverbs Explained*, 1967)

【参】To err is human, to forgive divine. / Don't make the same mistake twice. / No man is infallible.

【引】Even Homer sometimes nods. / Homer occasionally nodded. / Famous God Jove nods on occasion.

Liángyào kǔ kǒu lì yú bìng, zhōngyán nì ěr lì yú xíng

良药苦口利于病，忠言逆耳利于行

Voc. 良药 good medicine，苦口 bitter in taste，利于 good for，忠言 candid advice，逆耳 grate on the ear

Lit. Good medicine is bitter in taste but good for the disease; Candid advice grates on the ear but benefits conduct.

Exp. It is important to take the sincere advice even though it may be very unpleasant to hear.

Ex. 甲：这个教练够狠的。你听见过他训斥他的队员吗？

乙：他这个人的确不讲情面。但是良药苦口利于病，忠言逆耳利于行。

甲：你说得不错。为了出成绩，严格一点儿可能是必要的。但愿他的队员能够理解。

Quot. 达三哥觉得我的话不好听吗？良药苦口利于病，忠言逆耳利于行。要是我将来能够帮忙的话，我就不能不把你们的病根指出。（李劼人《大波》）

Cf. 好话不好听/严是爱，松是害，不管不教是祸害/辣椒辣口不辣心，好话刺耳出真情

Var. 良药苦口，忠言逆耳/良药苦口，乃是利病；忠言逆耳，乃是利行/良药苦口，忠言刺耳

Hard words break no bones

【义】严厉的话不会打折骨头。

【解】比喻应该能够接受措辞严厉的批评或建议。

【例】A：The coach is really cruel. Did you hear what he said to David?

B：Yeah, you're right, he is quite mean. However, **hard words break no bones**. All he wants is to push David to play harder.

A：Perhaps it is good for David. I hope he is calm and doesn't let what the coach says bother him.

【引】Soft words! They butter no parsnips ... Would you prefer hard ones? ... Hard words break no bones. (G. Nelson, *Charity's Child*, 1980)

【参】Sticks and stones may break my bones, but words will never hurt me. / Fine words butter no parsnips.

Liáng yán yí jù sāndōng nuǎn, èyǔ shāng rén liùyuè hán

良言一句三冬暖，恶语伤人六月寒

Voc. 良言 sweet words，恶语伤人 hurt people with rude language

Lit. Sweet words make people feel warm even in the winter-time, and abusive language hurts people and makes them feel cold even in summer.

Exp. People respond better to politeness and warmness than they do to rudeness or meanness.

Ex. 甲：最近我跟小李的关系越来越紧张。

乙：为什么？

甲：我们是室友，可是她的东西总是乱放。我没留情面，当着大家的面狠狠说了她几句。

乙：怪不得。良言一句三冬暖，恶语伤人六月寒。别人要是这样对你，你不生气才怪呢。

Quot. 李娇儿……见潘金莲对看月娘，骂他家千淫妇，万淫妇，暗暗怀恨在心。从此二人结仇，不在话下。正是甜言美语三冬暖，恶语伤人六月寒。（《金瓶梅词话》）

Cf. 好话一句暖人心/和气修条路，惹人筑堵墙/利人之言，暖如布帛；伤人之言，痛如刀戟/棍子伤骨，恶语伤心

Var. 好话一句三冬暖，恶语伤人六月寒/良言入耳三冬暖，恶语伤人六月寒

Honey catches more flies than vinegar

【义】用蜂蜜比用醋更容易抓住苍蝇。

【解】意指热情友善的态度比尖酸刻薄更容易被人们所接受。

【例】A：Sue，how did you get Dr. Walker to give you an extension on your paper?

B：I asked him nicely. **Honey catches more flies than vinegar**.

A：So by being pleasant，he gave you the extension. I would much rather deal with a pleasant individual over a grumpy one，too.

B：Friendly people are much easier to deal with.

【引】Generally speaking，you're going to catch a lot more flies with honey than with vinegar，as the saying goes. （Philip Friedman，*Inadmissible Evidence*）

【参】Tart words make no friends.

【引】You can catch more flies with honey than with vinegar. / A spoonful of honey will catch more flies than a gallon of vinegar. / You can catch more flies with sugar than vinegar.

Liǎng niǎo zài lín, bùrú yì niǎo zài shǒu

两鸟在林，不如一鸟在手

Voc. 鸟 bird，林 forest，不如 not as good as

Lit. One bird in the hand is better than two birds in the forest.

Exp. It is always better to have something than nothing at all, even though it is not so much as we have hoped for. It also means "to have a good grasp of one thing".

Ex. 甲：我想换个工作。现在这个工作我有点儿烦了。
乙：有希望吗？
甲：有两个公司收到了我的申请，他们让我等机会。
乙：其实你现在的工作挺不错的。两鸟在林，不如一鸟在手。还是先干好目前的工作吧。

Quot. 最稳当的办法，目前还是下乡去，……比较去分公司当小头目，是两鸟在林，不如一鸟在手的事。（张恨水《魍魉世界》）

Cf. 人心不足蛇吞象/天上的仙鹤，比不上手里的麻雀

Var. 二鸟在林，不如一鸟在手/一鸟在手，胜于两鸟在林

A bird in the hand is worth two in the bush

【义】双鸟在林不如一鸟在手。

【解】比喻尽管能得到的没有期望的那么多，但是总比没有好，而且以后还会有希望。

【例】A：It would be better if I could change my job.

B：Why?

A：I want to be closer to my home and have more vacation time.

B：Is that possible?

A：I heard that there are two companies that may have openings in the next few years.

B：Well, **a bird in the hand is worth two in the bush**. If I were you, I would be grateful to have a job.

【引】The antique dealer said I might get ten pounds for the vase if I took it up to London, but he himself wasn't prepared to give me more than five for it. A bird in hand, I thought, and accepted his offer. (R. Ridout & C. Witting, *English Proverbs Explained*, 1967)

【参】Half a loaf is better than no bread. / Half a bun is better than no cake. / Half a lie is better than no truth. / A living dog is better than a dead lion.

Mǎ shàn bèi rén qí, rén shàn bèi rén qī

马善被人骑，人善被人欺

Voc. 善 virtuous，骑 ride，欺 bully

Lit. A good horse is often ridden by some people and a kind-hearted person is easily cheated by others.

Exp. It suggests that a person shouldn't be too soft and timid.

Ex. 甲：我的室友从来都不收拾房间，昨天他还让我给他洗衣服。
乙：他难道没有手吗？
甲：我觉得同学应该互相帮助，所以总是主动为他做事。
乙：马善被人骑，人善被人欺。你太老实了，别人就会占你便宜。

Quot. 他老实善道的，树叶掉了怕砸头，蚂蚁过路急抬脚。唉，马善有人骑，人善有人欺，高大泉经常把他欺负得像皮球，踢来踢去。（浩然《金光大道》）

Cf. 软的欺，硬的怕/人软被人欺，鸟软被猎欺/胆小没有将军做

Var. 人善被人欺，马善被人骑/马老实有人骑，人老实有人欺

A low hedge is easily leaped over

【义】矮篱笆容易翻跃过去。

【解】过分老实容易让人得利。常指穷人往往受欺负。

【例】A：It was pay day yesterday. Did you get your paycheck?

B：Not yet. My boss said he was tight of money.

A：That is not an excuse. Remember, **a low hedge is easily leaped over**. If I were you, I would ask for the paycheck tomorrow.

【参】He who makes himself honey will be eaten by the bees.

【异】Where the hedge is lowest, everyone, including the devil, leaps over. / Where the hedge is thin, men will see through it.

Méiyǒu bú tòufēng de qiáng

没有不透风的墙

Voc. 透风 let in air，墙 wall

Lit. No wall is windtight.

Exp. Even though you are outside in an apparently empty landscape, someone may be eavesdropping on you.

Ex. 甲：我有点儿事要告诉你。
乙：什么事？
甲：不能在楼道里讲。要知道，没有不透风的墙。
乙：那去哪儿？
甲：放学以后，等人都走了再谈吧。
乙：其实，不管什么地方或者什么时候，秘密总是会让人知道的。你干脆现在就告诉我吧。

Quot. 这你就不用瞒我了，我什么都知道，没有不透风的墙。（戴厚英《人啊，人》）

Cf. 天有眼，墙有耳/隔墙有耳/要想人不知，除非己莫为

Var. 没有不透风的篱笆/世上没有不透风的墙/纸里包不住火，没有不透风的墙

Fields have eyes, and woods have ears

【义】土地有眼，树木有耳。

【解】比喻任何消息总会有人知道。

【例】A：Julie，I have something to tell you.

B：Ok，what is it?

A：Not here in the hallway where the **fields have eyes，and the woods have ears**.

B：Where then?

A：I'll tell you after school when there aren't so many people around to hear what I need to tell you.

B：I think someone will know what you tell me no matter when and where. However，I'll see you after school.

【引】Heedful of the old saying，that fields have eyes and woods have ears. She looked carefully round her before she laid her hand on the gate. (J. Weyman，*Starvecrow Farm*，1905)

【参】Walls have ears. / Woods have tongues. / If walls have ears，then woods have eyes.

Méiyǒu jīngāngzuànr, bù lǎn cíqì huór

没有金刚钻儿，不揽瓷器活儿

Voc. 金刚 diamond，钻儿 drill，揽 take over，瓷器 chinaware，活儿 job

Lit. Don't take the chinaware job if you haven't a diamond drill.

Exp. Don't take the job if you are not able to do it, and leave it to those who can handle it without difficulties.

Ex. 甲：你看，我最近睡不好觉，头发都开始掉了。

乙：怎么搞的？你最好去看看医生。

甲：大夫也帮不了我！自从我买了股票以后，一直特别紧张。市场行情每天忽上忽下，我真担心可能一下子把钱都丢光。

乙：谁能把握准股市的行情？没有金刚钻儿，不揽瓷器活儿。要是我是你的话，我会把股票都卖了，把钱放进银行。既然你承受不了这样的压力，你就应该让自己解脱出来。

甲：谢谢你，我会考虑的。

Quot. 虽然有的名词儿不懂，可也听着好听，怪不得他敢代表共产党到这儿来，这真是没有金刚钻儿，不揽瓷器活儿啊！（刘流《烈火金刚》）

Cf. 有多大本钱，做多大生意/不是撑船手，休来弄竹竿/没有下唇，就不该揽着箫吹/没有空城计，退不了司马懿/人贵有自知之明

Var. 没有金刚钻，别揽这瓷器活/没有金刚钻，莫揽大瓷活/没有金刚钻，揽不来瓷器活/没有金刚钻，怎会揽瓷器活

If you can't stand the heat, get out of the kitchen

【义】要是你怕热，就到厨房外边去。

【解】一个人如果不能承受某种特殊情况或环境的压力，最好离开，量力而为。

【例】A：You know what, I can't sleep well recently, I'm starting to lose my hair.

B：How come? You had better go to see your doctor.

A：Well, my doctor can't help me. I have been so nervous ever since I bought this stock. The market goes up and down every day. I'm afraid that I might suddenly lose most of my money.

B：Nobody can predict the market. **If you can't stand the heat, get out of the kitchen**. I would sell my stocks and put my money into the bank if I were you. Since you can't tolerate the pressures, you should remove yourself from this situation.

A：I will think about it. Thanks.

【引】Property people argue that hoteliers are not facing the facts of economic life, and that if they cannot stand the heat they should get out of the kitchen. (*Financial Times*, 1970)

If you can't stand the heat, get out of the kitchen. That's what tough-talking politicians say.... (*Washington Post*, 1989)

【参】If you can't run with the big dogs, stay under the porch. / If you're gonna run with the big dogs, you can't pee like a puppy.

【异】If you don't like the heat, stay out of the kitchen.

Móu shì zài rén, chéng shì zài tiān

谋事在人，成事在天

Voc. 谋事 plan matters，成事 accomplish something

Lit. The planning lies with man, but the outcome with Heaven.

Exp. We should try our best, but be ready to whatever the result is.

Ex. 甲：听天气预报说，明晚有大风暴，我们得赶快加固河堤。

乙：只有一天时间，来得及吗？

甲：谋事在人，成事在天，我们尽最大的努力。但是这次风暴到底有多大，就看运气了。

乙：好，我们赶快行动吧。

Quot. 谁知天不做美，偏偏到了十月间，变雄为雌，又产下一位公主。这正叫做谋事在人，成事在天呢！（蔡东藩《慈禧太后演义》）

Cf. 不问收获，只问耕耘/不以成败论英雄

Var. 谋事在人成在天/谋事虽在人，成事还在天

Hope for the best and prepare for the worst

【义】抱最好的希望，做最坏的准备。

【解】表示人应该一方面朝最好的方向去努力，另一方面却要做好最坏的心理准备。

【例】A：Mom, why are you packing like we are going away for the weekend?

B：There is a bad storm coming, and we are packing just in case we need to go to a shelter.

A：I am scared, and I don't want to leave the house.

B：I don't want to leave either. We are **hoping for the best and preparing for the worst**. This way if the storm does come, we are ready; but if it doesn't, then there is no harm done by packing a few things.

A：It is a good idea. We just do what we should, and let's see what will happen.

【引】Hope for the best, but prepare for the worst. According to Capt. Fred Crocker of the Hartford, Com., Fire Department, "People who have prepared for a fire are much more likely to survive than those who haven't." (*Reader's Digest*, 1992)

【参】Hope springs eternal in the human breast.

【异】Hope for the best and expect the worst. / Hope for the best, and trust in God. / Look for the best and expect the worst.

Mùjiang duō le gài wāi fáng

木匠多了盖歪房

Voc. 木匠 carpenter，盖 build，歪 crooked

Lit. If there are too many carpenters，they will build a crooked house.

Exp. If there are too many people working on the same project，the job won't be done properly. It is used in any situation where more than the appropriate number of people for the task get involved.

Ex. 甲：哎，你怎么啦？

乙：现在我真不知道怎么办。原来让我负责安排明年冬天的会议，对我来说这完全不是问题。可是后来经理以为我需要帮忙，就派了一帮人来给我提建议。现在这些人里有不少跟我意见不同。

甲：我知道，“木匠多了盖歪房”。

乙：可不是！请几个人提点建议倒没关系，意见太多了就不知道听谁的。太多人做一件事，结果肯定好不了。

Quot. 厨子多了做坏汤，木匠多了盖歪房。（《英汉谚语辞典》，Lanbridge Press，1998）

Cf. 人多手杂，嘴多口杂/一个和尚挑水吃，两个和尚抬水吃，三个和尚没水吃/人多乱，龙多旱，鸡多不下蛋/人多手脚乱/天上星多月不明，地上人多心不平

Too many cooks spoil the broth

【义】厨子多了煮坏汤。

【解】表示如果太多的人去做同一件事，反而会把这件事搞糟。

【例】A：Hey，Gina，what's going on?

B：Oh，I'm really frustrated at the moment. I was given responsibility for organizing the next winter conference，which is no problem for me，but then my manager thought that I might need some help，so he assigned a whole team of people to give me their input. Now I have all these people who are trying to give me input on something they can't even agree about.

A：I know what you mean：**Too many cooks spoil the broth**.

B：Yes，it's true. Although it's okay to have a little input from others，too many opinions are like too many ingredients added to a soup by too many cooks. When too many people are involved in a project，the result will be confusing.

【引】"It was a great mistake to think that administration was improved by taking on more administrators ... 'Too many cooks spoil the broth'." (*Guardian*，7，Nov.，1979)

The old adage "too many cooks spoil the sauce" will be tested when the chefs participating in Tastes of the Nation ... (*Time Off*，1995)

【参】Half-a-dozen gentlemen aboard one ship are as bad as two kings of Brentford. / Three things in a bag，and the bag is in the trash. (Spanish) /The more cooks the worse pottage.

【异】Too many cooks spoil the stew. / Too many cooks spoil the sauce.

Nì shuǐ xíng zhōu, bú jìn zé tuì

逆水行舟，不进则退

Voc. 逆水 go against the current，舟 boat，则 then

Lit. A boat sails against the current — either forging ahead or falling behind.

Exp. We must make progress and we must improve now. Otherwise, we'll fall behind.

Ex. 甲：今年的比赛第一名是没希望了，我的目标是保住去年的第二名。

乙：别忘了，逆水行舟，不进则退。你如果不想争第一，恐怕连第二也保不住。

甲：你别小看我。我一定拿个冠军回来！

Quot. 俗话说："逆水行舟，不进则退"。果不其然，在卫平决心自暴自弃之后，他又惹下一场大祸。（朱小明《棋坛旋风聂卫平》）

Cf. 时间好像东流水，只能流去不流回/年怕中秋月怕半

Var. 逆水行船，不进便退

If you don't improve today, you'll grow worse tomorrow

【义】如果你今天没有进步，那么明天会更差。

【解】表示一个人每天都应该有所进取，否则就等于是在后退。

【例】A：I'm so tired that I want to have a vacation.

B：Don't you know the competition is coming soon?

A：Yes, I do. It will be fine as long as I can keep my second place.

B：**If you don't improve today, you'll grow worse tomorrow**

If you don't work hard every day, you'll fail in the competition.

【参】If not us, who? If not now, when? / If you lose your time, you cannot get money or gain. / If you must fly, fly well. / He who doesn't gain loses. / He who doesn't advance loses ground.

Niǎo yào yǒu chìbǎng, rén yào yǒu lǐxiǎng

鸟要有翅膀，人要有理想

Voc. 翅膀 wing，理想 ideal

Lit. A bird needs wings, and a person must have his ideals.

Exp. Everyone must have his goals and hopes to achieve. Otherwise, he will be lost and lifeless.

Ex. 甲：几个星期不见，你怎么瘦多了？

乙：高考落榜，工作又找不到，我觉得自己真是个废物。

甲：千万别泄气。鸟要有翅膀，人要有理想。你不是喜欢文艺吗？可以搞业余创作呀。

乙：听你一说，我好像又找到了希望，插上了理想的翅膀……

甲：行了行了，你别说创作就创作起来了。

Quot. 鸟最要紧的是两只翅膀，不然就不能飞翔；人最重要的是树立理想，否则就无所作为，一事无成。（王卿、刘书祥《谚语小词典》）

Cf. 人凭志气虎凭威/人无志，刀无钢/人若没有大目标，一根稻草压弯腰/得志一条龙，失志一条虫/菜无心死，人无志亡

Hope deferred makes the heart sick

【义】希望迟迟不能实现会使人心烦意乱。

【解】表示如果一个人失去了希望和努力的目标就会失去精神的支柱和生活的意义。

【例】A：Bill doesn't have any hope that Ann will get better and be released from the hospital.

B：I know. He is so sad and depressed. I wish there was something we could do for him, because **hope deferred makes the heart sick**.

A：Well, he has been waiting a long time for Ann to come home, and she hasn't yet. I am not sure there is much we can do to ease his sadness.

B：Perhaps we can hope for him.

【引】If hope deferred makes the heart sick, despair is a poor counselor also. (*Observer*, 1981)

【参】Hope and have. / Hope holds up the head. / Hope to the end. / Hope springs eternal. / Hope keeps the heart from breaking.

【异】Hope deferred makes the heart sick; but when the desire comes, it is a tree of life. / Hopes delayed hang the heart upon tenterhooks.

Nìng zài zhí zhōng qǔ, bú xiàng qū zhōng qiú

宁在直中取，不向曲中求

Voc. 宁 would rather，直 straight，曲 curved，求 seek

Lit. It's better to strive for something in a straight rather than a curved way.

Exp. It is better to be straightforward when taking an action, rather than indirect or dishonest although it may be profitable for a while.

Ex. 甲：这项工程要招标了，听说竞争很厉害。

乙：我认识负责招标的张主任，你要不要先去看望他一下，拉拉关系？

甲：我不愿意这样做。宁在直中取，不向曲中求。

乙：好吧，看你的本事了。

Quot. 岂可曲中而取鱼乎！非丈夫之所为也。吾宁在直中取，不向曲中求。（《封神演义》）

Cf. 不做亏心事，不怕鬼叫门/人直有人合，路直有人行/一正避三邪/清水见底，明镜明心

Var. 宁可直中取，不可曲中求

Honesty is the best policy

【义】诚实才是上策。

【解】意指为人处事最好的方法莫过于诚实和正直。

【例】A：Ms. Wilson, I broke your car window. I am very sorry, I didn't think the baseball was going to hit it. I would like to pay for it.

B：Tom, thank you for telling me the truth. I appreciate your honesty. **Honesty is the best policy**

A：What do you mean?

B：Well, you were honest and told me the truth. When you are honest, others appreciate it.

A：So you are not mad at me?

B：No, now go to play ball.

【引】Of course the official rule of the market is that honesty is the best policy — or, at least, that any deal mutually beneficial to both buyer and seller requires honesty. (*New York Times Magazine*, 1995)

【参】Honesty is the first step to greatness. / Honesty pays.

【异】Honesty is by far the best policy. / Honesty is the safest policy. / Truth is always the best policy. / Honesty is the best policy, though it may not pay the largest dividends.

Pá de yuè gāo, shuāi de yuè zhòng

爬得越高，摔得越重

Voc. 爬 climb，摔 fall，重 heavily

Lit. The higher the climb，the nastier the fall.

Exp. Don't be too ambitious or aggressive. Realize your own limitations，otherwise，there is a penalty of ambition.

Ex. 甲：你听说了吗，小张刚来公司几个月就当上副总经理了。
乙：当然听说了，他这个人特别会往上爬。
甲：有时候，爬得越高，摔得越重。
乙：可不是。我看，你有点儿忌妒他，对不对？

Quot. 大凤很少说话。这一回她开口了："小心呀，妹妹，人都说爬得越高，摔得越疼呀！"（老舍《鼓书艺人》）

Cf. 出头的椽子先烂/位尊身危，名高忌起/位高多谤

Var. 爬得越高，跌得越惨/爬得高，跌得重/捧得高，跌得重/捧得高高的，摔得扁扁的/攀得高，跌得重

The higher the fool, the greater the fall

【义】傻瓜爬得越高，摔得越重。

【解】表示如果不适当地追求某个目标，那么往往会越走离目标越远。

【例】A：Do you know that John has been promoted as the manager? He has worked in our company for less than three months.

B：It was said that he likes to fish for fame and compliments.

A：I think **the higher the fool, the greater the fall.**

B：I agree. You are jealous of him, aren't you?

【引】The great expectations cost Norr Turner his job. And the attending soap opera quality made Dan Snyder a villainous stick figure across the nation. The lesson is obvious: The higher you attempt to climb, the more your behind shows. (*Washington Post*, 2000)

【参】The highest branch is not the safest roost. /Uneasy lies the head that wears a crown. /The higher the monkey climbs, the more he shows his tail. / High regions are never without storms.

【异】The higher they rise, the steeper they fall. / The higher you climb, the greater will be your fall. / The highest climbers have the greatest falls. / The highest tree has the greatest fall. / The highest trees abide the sharpest winds.

Qiān lǐ sòng émáo, lǐ qīng qíngyì zhòng

千里送鹅毛，礼轻情义重

Voc. 鹅 goose，毛 feather，礼 gift，轻 light，情义 feeling，重 heavy

Lit. The gift itself may be light as a goose feather, but sent from a thousand *li* away, it conveys deep feeling.

Exp. Don't judge a gift by its value. It should be appreciated even if it is small / light in value, since the friendship is priceless.

Ex. 甲：周末我们一起去逛商店吧。快过年了，你打算送你朋友什么礼物？

乙：你难道不知道？我现在是穷学生。我想从网上下载几首歌儿给他发去。

甲：你可真够小气的！

乙：千里送鹅毛，礼轻情义重。他要是嫌我的礼物不好，恐怕我们就不会是朋友了。

Quot. 俗话说"千里送鹅毛，礼轻情义重"，她不过是想表表自己的一片心意。（顾笑言《哑巴西施》）

Cf. 千里寄鹅毛，物轻人意重/千里送毫毛，礼轻情义重

Don't look a gift horse in the mouth

【义】不要去看别人送给你的马的嘴巴（以得知马的年龄）。

【解】告诫人们不要去挑剔别人送的礼物。

【例】A：I didn't know you owned a car. Where did you get it from?

B：My elder sister gave it to me.

A：It seems very nice. You must be very lucky.

B：There are plenty of things wrong with this car that you don't know about until you drive it . I suspect that's why she no longer wanted it.

A：**Don't look a gift horse in the mouth**. If I were you, I would feel grateful.

B：I guess you're right. I shouldn't look for defects in gifts.

【引】Charities are usually not so picky about donors and they don't look gift horses in the mouth. (*Forbes*, 1983)

【异】A gift horse should not be looked in the mouth. / Look not a gift horse in the mouth. / Never look a gift loris in the eye. / Never look a gift horse in the mouth. / Don't look at a gift horse's teeth.

Qiáng àn niútóu chī bu dé cǎo

强按牛头吃不得草

Voc. 强 by force，按 push down，牛 ox，草 grass

Lit. You can't make an ox eat by forcing his head to the grass.

Exp. You can't force someone to do what you want him to do.

Ex. 甲：你听说公司的退休计划了吗？
乙：还没有。
甲：他们打算提供一些优惠，让那些年龄大的工人提前退休。
乙：你觉得老周会提前退休吗？
甲：说不好。有些优惠的确挺吸引人。但是俗话说，强按牛头吃不得草。说到底，不管这些优惠多么吸引人，最终还是得由这些人根据自己的情况来决定。

Quot. 陈国斌知道蒋丛森是个强按牛头不吃草的角色，……忙对他眨眨眼睛，示意他不必当真。（房群等《剑与盾》）

Cf. 强扭的瓜不甜/抢着不是买卖，拉着不是亲戚/以理服人心服，以力服人身服

Var. 强按牛头不吃草/强按牛头不喝水/牛不喝水难按角

You can lead a horse to water, but you can't make him drink

【义】你可以把马牵到水边，但是你不能硬让它喝水。

【解】比喻你可以给别人提供建议，但是不可以强迫别人接受。

【例】A：Did you hear what the management is planning to do?

B：No, please tell me.

A：They are going to offer some incentives to try to get some of the older workers to take early retirement.

B：Do you think our friend Joe will take early retirement? He seems to really enjoy his job.

A：I don't know. Some of the incentives they're going to offer are pretty attractive but it's like the old saying goes：**You can lead a horse to water, but you can't make him drink**. Ultimately, no matter how attractive the incentives are, people will have to make their own decisions.

【引】You can lead a horse to water, but the question is, can you make it drink? Once you get the adults in, can you keep them interested? (*Wall Street Journal*)

You can lead your son to college but you can't make him think. (*Jewish Press*)

【异】You can take a horse to water, but you can't make him drink.

Qīnqi péngyou yuǎn lái xiāng

亲戚朋友远来香

Voc. 亲戚 relative，香 fragrant / welcome

Lit. Relatives and friends who come from far away are very welcome.

Exp. In human relationships, distance may lead to respect, and familiarity can cause contempt.

Ex. 甲：我真讨厌给他做事。以前我觉得他是一个值得尊敬的人，但是给他工作以后改变了我的看法。

乙：俗话说，亲戚朋友远来香。

甲：我想是这样。你对一个人越了解，就越容易发现他的缺点。

Quot. 老人古语说得好，亲家朋友远来香，别总在眼皮底下，舌头挨着牙，总碰着就不好了。（董玉振《聪明的糊涂人》）

Var. 亲戚远来香，隔房高打墙/亲戚远来香

Familiarity breeds contempt

【义】熟识导致轻视。

【解】表示对某人或某事熟悉和了解之后，人们往往会变得不在乎甚至看不起对方。

【例】A：I hate working for Wayne. I used to think he was a pleasant person, but working for him has changed my opinion.

B：I guess **familiarity breeds contempt**.

A：I'll say it does. I am learning the longer I know him, the less I like him.

B：So he is not so friendly and social as he appears to be in public when he is in the office.

A：I know that's true!

【引】Often if you stick around the same company or the same city too long, you become old hat ... People think they know everything about you ... The new way to say it is, "They've seen you in underwear." The old way is, "Familiarity breeds contempt." (*Esquire*, 1988)

【参】No man is a hero to his valet. /A prophet is not without honor save in his own country. / Respect is greater from a distance. / Distance leads enchantment to the view.

【异】Desperation breeds contempt. /Familiarity breeds a variety of contempt. / Familiarity breeds indifference. / Nothing breeds contempt like unfamiliarity.

Qíngrén yǎn li chū Xīshī

情人眼里出西施

Voc. 情人 lover，西施 a famous beauty in the state of Yue during the late Spring and Autumn period of China

Lit. Beauty lies in the lover's eyes.

Exp. What seems ordinary or ugly to people might seem very beautiful to their sweethearts. (Mainly used for women.)

Ex. 甲：看见墙上那张照片了吗？漂亮吧？
乙：我倒不觉得。老实说，挺难看的。
甲：什么？我怎么越看越觉得漂亮？
乙：每个人的眼光都不同。情人眼里出西施。看来，你喜欢上照片里的那个人了，对不对？

Quot. 俗话说："情人眼里出西施。"只要有了纯真的爱情，即使长相差点，你们也会爱得火热。（卢晓峰《爱情》）

Var. 情人眼里有西施/情人眼内出西施

Beauty is in the eye of the beholder

【义】美丽出自关注你的人的眼中。

【解】人们对事物的评价往往是不同的。某些人认为一般甚至丑陋的东西对另一些人来说则是美丽的。

【例】A: Look at that painting over there. Isn't it beautiful?

B: I don't think it's very beautiful at all. In fact it's ugly.

A: Well, remember: **Beauty is in the eye of the beholder**

B: You're right. Each person sees things differently and also has a different opinion of what is beautiful and what is not beautiful.

【引】A miracle is in the eye of the beholder, thought Hisako. She'd just seen a westbound jet fly nearly across the sky and then, with a sudden turn, fly back to the east. (*New York Times*, 1992)

【参】Miracle is in the eye of the beholder. / Evil is in the eye of the beholder. / Old age is in the eye of the beholder.

Rén bù kě mào xiàng, hǎishuǐ bù kě dǒu liáng

人不可貌相，海水不可斗量

Voc. 貌 appearance，相 tell，斗 a unit of measure for grain，量 mete

Lit. As a man can't be judged by his appearance, the ocean can't be measured with a *dou*.

Exp. It is important to judge a man by his character rather than by his appearance.

Ex. 甲：你看到你们的新主管了吗？

乙：还没有。但是我肯定知道他是哪个人。

甲：为什么？

乙：我刚才看见一个人从办公室出来，他穿着剪裁得体的西装，提着一个文件包，等电梯的时候，还看了好几次表，看来是去参加一个重要的会议，那肯定是他了。

甲：人不可貌相，海水不可斗量。那个人是你主管的助手，你的主管是个女的。看来，光看外表有时会上当的。

Quot. 常言道："人不可貌相，海水不可斗量。"不要看他其貌不扬，其实，他是一个非同凡响的人物。（李良杰《月季情》）

Cf. 包子有肉不在褶儿上/光头圆顶的不一定都是和尚

Var. 人不可貌相，水不可斗量/人无貌相，水无斗量/人不可貌取

Clothes do not make the man

【义】人靠的不是服饰。

【解】表示判断一个人不是根据服装，而是人自身的素质、性格等。

【例】A：Have you met the supervisor yet?

B：Not yet, although I'm sure I know which person he is.

A：How is that?

B：Well, I saw a very well-dressed man in a designer suit carrying a leather attaché case come out of that office over there. He kept glancing at his watch as he waited for the elevator. It seemed that he was heading to an important meeting.

A：I'm sure you've heard the saying：**Clothes do not make the man**. That person is an assistant to your supervisor, who, I might add, is a woman. Just because a person dresses a certain way doesn't necessarily make it safe for someone else to make assumptions. Looks can be deceiving.

【引】I saw Howard the other day in a costume store. He was renting a suit of armor for a costume ball. ... Doesn't he know that clothes do not make the man? (H. Collis, *101 American English Proverbs*, 1992)

【参】The tailor makes the man. / Fine feathers make fine birds.

Rén kào yī zhuāng, fó kào jīn zhuāng

人靠衣装，佛靠金装

Voc. 靠 rely on，装 clothes，佛 Buddha

Lit. As man needs fine clothes, Buddha needs a gilt statue.

Exp. If you dress elegantly, people will think you are elegant. （It can be used ironically to suggest that even though someone dresses well, he or she is not a high-class person.）

Ex. 甲：你们店里最好的丝绸在哪儿？我女儿要参加毕业晚会，我想给她做套旗袍。

乙：就在那边，但非常贵。

甲：没关系。你知道“人靠衣装，佛靠金装”。我想把我女儿打扮成晚会上最漂亮的姑娘。

乙：我明白。等她穿上这套旗袍，一定又漂亮又高雅。

Quot. 虽然如此，佛是金装，人是衣装，打扮是极要紧的。（沈自晋《望湖亭传奇》）

Cf. 人靠衣服马靠鞍/三分长相七分打扮/人靠一张皮，木靠一层漆/人是衣装，马是鞍装/人配衣裳马配鞍，天仙也怕配穷酸/人是衣裳马是鞍

Var. 花须叶衬，佛要金装

Fine feathers make fine birds

【义】人在衣裳马在鞍。

【解】比喻有好的外表或精神才能有好的内在。

【例】A：I am looking for your best silk material to sew a dress for my daughter's prom.

B：Our best silks are over there, but they are very expensive.

A：No matter, you know, **fine feathers make fine birds**. I want only the best for my daughter.

B：I understand you want the best quality silk for your quality daughter. I am sure she will be as beautiful and elegant as her new silk gown.

【引】She's all dressed up and nowhere to go. Nowadays it takes more than fine feathers to make a fine bird. (Gregory Titelman, *Popular Proverbs and Sayings*, 1999)

【参】All that glitters is not gold. /Appearances are deceiving.

【异】Fair feathers make fair fowl. / It's not the feather that makes the bird. (注：有些谚语与 Fine feathers make fine birds 意思相反，但是同时存在。)

Rén zài ǎi yán xià, bù dé bù dī tóu

人在矮檐下，不得不低头

Voc. 矮 low，檐 eaves

Lit. One has to hang his head under low eaves.

Exp. Whoever facing an unfavorable circumstances must make concessions to survive.

Ex. 甲：马主任最近也下岗了？
乙：听说她找了个当保姆的工作。
甲：人在矮檐下，不得不低头啊。
乙：她还要供女儿上大学，不得不如此啊。

Quot. 唉！这种年头，凡事忍为高，古人说："人在矮檐下，谁敢不低头！"（马烽等《吕梁英雄传》）

Cf. 人穷低了三分志

Var. 人在矮檐下，不得不低头/在人矮檐下，怎敢不低头

Beggars can't be choosers

【义】讨饭难拣嘴。

【解】处于不利和劣势的人只能接受现实，顺应时势。

【例】A：Have you seen Jeff?

B：Yes, he's at my apartment. He had a big assignment that he had to finish up. I wanted to use my computer last night, but he begged me to let him use it instead. He eventually finished his work around 3：00 am, but he complained about my computer the whole time, "It's too slow. Why don't you get a better computer? Don't you have a better program than this one I'm using?" When he finished working, he asked to spend the night and then complained about his bed being uncomfortable. He made me quite angry.

A：It sounds like he was being quite unreasonable. He should know that **beggars can't be choosers**. Without your help he would have had no computer to use. It is impolite to ask someone a favor and then complain about what is given to you.

【引】I don't pretend I don't miss my garden. But there, beggars can't be choosers. (O. Mills, *Death Enters Lists*)

【参】He who pays the piper calls the tune. / Never look a gift horse in the mouth.

【异】Beggars must not be choosers.

Sān ge chòu píjiang, còu ge Zhūgě Liàng

三个臭皮匠，凑个诸葛亮

Voc. 臭 stinking，皮匠 cobbler，凑 gather together，诸葛亮 a statesman and strategist in the period of the Three Kingdoms (220 ~ 280)，now a symbol of great wisdom in Chinese folklore

Lit. Three stinky (not well educated) cobblers with their wits combined equal Zhuge Liang the mastermind.

Exp. It is a resource of great wisdom to have another person's opinion or advice even though the person may have a lower social status.

Ex. 甲：唉，我的脑子都空了。我的报告下星期五就得交了，可是我现在连一半都还没写完呢。

乙：我能帮什么忙吗？

甲：如果你能帮忙就太好了。三个臭皮匠，凑个诸葛亮。

乙：当然啦，有时候几个人把各自的想法凑起来，问题就容易解决了。

甲：真谢谢你了。

Quot. “三个臭皮匠，顶个诸葛亮，人多主意高。再说，活是靠大伙的，他们自己说定的，还能不干？”（草明《原动力》）

Cf. 人多出圣人/人多出韩信/一人不敌二人智/一人计短，二人计长

Var. 三个臭皮匠，合成一个诸葛亮/三个缝皮匠，比个诸葛亮/三个臭皮匠，抵个诸葛亮/三个臭皮匠，当个诸葛亮

Two heads are better than one

【义】一人计短，两人计长。

【解】集中大家的智慧和力量比一个单独做要好。

【例】A：Oh! My gosh! My brain is all dried up! The deadline for my proposal is next Friday, but I haven't finished half of it yet.

B：Is there something that I can help with?

A：That will be great if you can. **Two heads are better than one**. I can't figure out the cost for data collection. Consequently I don't know how big of the budget I'll need to apply for.

B：I see. You know I could offer some suggestions if you like. It's sometimes easier to solve problems when two people pool their resources and ideas.

A：Hey, I'd really appreciate your help. I believe two of us working together can certainly solve the problem faster than me working alone.

【引】Two heads are better than one. So, do two hearts that beat as one. (J. Dixon, *Horoscope*, 1993)

Two paychecks are better than one. In 1978, American family in 5 had income totaling more than $25,000, and in two thirds of those families at least 2 members worked. (Mike Feinsilber & William B. Mead, *American Averages*, 1998)

【参】Four eyes see more than two. / Two eyes can see more than one. / Two hands are better than one. / Two wits are better than one.

Sān sī ér hòu xíng

三思而后行

Voc. Think thrice before you act.

Lit. Consider all the aspects of a situation before you take any action. / Don't make any serious decision rashly.

Ex. 甲：我毕业以后打算去国外工作。我听说外国公司给职工的福利好一些。再说，我也喜欢旅行。

乙：主意还不错，但是你应该三思而后行。据我所知，住在外国也并不容易。你不但要适应一个陌生的环境，而且还得会说那个国家的语言。另外，跟亲戚朋友长期分开的滋味也不好受。要是我的话，我会把各方面的情况考虑清楚以后再说。

甲：有道理，这件事儿我要再想想。

Quot. 季文子三思而后行。（《论语·公冶长》）

君子有三思而不可不思也。（《荀子·法行》）

Cf. 一念之差，终生之累/一着不慎，满盘皆输/大意失荆州/小心无大错/事要前思，免劳后悔

Var. 三思而缓行/事不三思，终有后悔/棋子一步一步走，事有三思而后行

Look before you leap

【义】看好再跳。

【解】做任何事以前都要先考虑好各方面的情况。

【例】A：I'm thinking of going abroad to work after my graduation. It was said that foreign companies can provide better benefit to their employees. In addition, I like traveling.

B：It's not a bad idea. However, you should **look before you leap**. As far as I know, living in a foreign country is not easy. Not only do you need to make a lot of adjustment to a foreign environment, but you should also be able to speak the native language. In addition, it is hard to be away from your relatives and friends for a long time. If I were you, I would consider all aspects of a situation before I take any action.

A：You are right. I'll think about it again.

【引】Do you remember the rousing slogan which the Prime Minister gave the voters ... on the eve of the last General Election? ... Look Before You Leap.

(C. Mackenzie, *Red Tapeworm*, 1941)

Whatever his leaders told him to do, he did. They told him to look before he leaped, and he always looked before he leaped. (Joseph Heller, *Catch-22*, 1961)

【参】Slow and steady wins the race. / Marry in haste, repent at leisure. / One step at a time. / If you can't be good, be careful.

【异】Look before you leap and think before you speak. / Think twice before you leap.

Shān zhōng wú lǎohǔ, hóuzi chēng dàwáng

山中无老虎，猴子称大王

Voc. 老虎 tiger，猴子 monkey，称 call

Lit. When the tiger is absent from the mountain, the monkey proclaims himself king.

Exp. Someone will dominate when the authority or master is away.

Ex. 甲：哎，你急急忙忙去哪儿？

乙：我正担心我的孩子呢。三个孩子自己待在家里，恐怕会惹祸的。

甲：可不是！山中无老虎，猴子称大王。如果没有家长或老师在那儿看着，他们就会想怎么做就怎么做的。

乙：是啊。这正是我担心的。我最好早点儿回家看看吧。再见……

Quot. 海婴已以第一名在幼稚园毕业，其实亦不过“山中无老虎，猴子称大王”而已。(鲁迅《书信集·致母亲》)

Var. 山中无好汉，猢狲称霸王/山上无老虎，猴子称大王

In the country of the blind, the one-eyed man is king

【义】在盲人的国度里，有一只眼的人就是国王。

【解】比喻尽管有的人的本领不是最高的，但是如果在一定环境中他的能力高于别人，那么他就会取得特殊的地位。

【例】A：John，why are you in a hurry?

B：I am worried about my kids. I left all three of them at home alone. They might get into trouble.

A：Well，you know，**in the country of the blind，the one-eyed man is king.** When an authority figure is not there to lay down some rules，your eldest child will be the leader.

B：Yes，that's what I worry about. I had better go back home early to check on them. Bye-bye.

【引】It's enough to make you cry to see how bad most people are at their jobs. If you can do a half-assed job of anything you're a one-eyed man in the kingdom of the blind.（Kurt Vonnegut，Jr.，*Player Piano*，1952）

【参】When the cat's away，the mice may play.

【异】In the kingdom（or land）of the blind，the one-eyed man is king.

Shàng liáng bú zhèng xià liáng wāi

上梁不正下梁歪

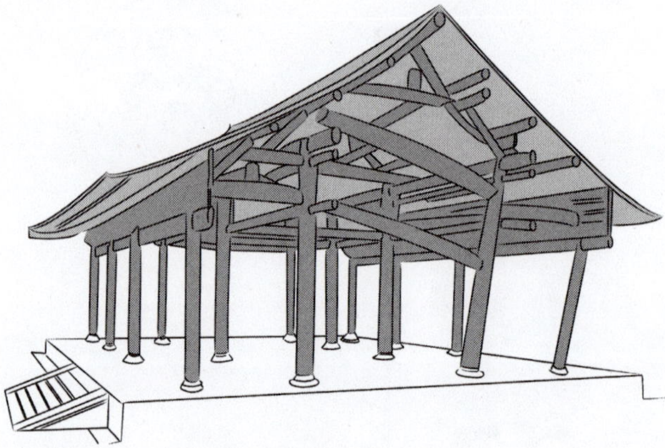

Voc. 上梁 upper beam，下梁 lower beam，歪 aslant

Lit. If the upper beam is not straight, the lower ones will go aslant.

Exp. Those below always behave like those above do.

Ex. 甲：你知道吗？这孩子特别爱撒谎，不光骗同学，连老师也敢骗。

乙：是吗？上梁不正下梁歪。问题学生背后往往是问题家庭。

甲：最近我打算家访一次，跟他父母一起教育他。

Quot. 一个副部长这样干，怪不得他分管的铁道部运输局的班子基本上烂掉了。上梁不正下梁歪，中梁不正房子塌下来。（何华《公生明，廉生威》）

Cf. 一头坏驴，带坏一圈马/跟上啥人学啥人，跟上巫婆学跳神

Var. 上边梁正下边直/上梁不整下梁差/上梁弗正，下梁参差/上梁不正下梁歪，根子不好葫芦赖

The fish always stinks from the head

【义】鱼要腐烂头先臭。

【解】比喻如果领导者行为不端，下属也会跟着效仿。

【例】A：Do you know that Steven's company has declared bankrupcy?

B：I heard the company's CEO took bribes, and a few managers were also corrupt.

A：No wonder. **The fish always stinks from the head.**

B：Exactly. When the head part is rotten, the rest will follow soon.

【引】"The fish," as the saying goes, "always stinks from the head downwards." Last Sunday we deplored Mr. Michael Foot's liking for the street politics of matches and "demos". Since then, a hundred labors MPs ... have followed their leader's example. (*Sunday Telegraph*, May 16, 1981)

【异】The fish always stinks from the head downwards. / If a fish smells, look at his head. /Fish begins to stink at the head.

Shào zhuàng bù nǔlì, lǎo dà tú shāngbēi

少壮不努力，老大徒伤悲

Voc. 少壮 young and vigorous，徒 in vain，伤悲 sorrowful

Lit. If one doesn't exert oneself in youth，one will regret it in old age.

Exp. Don't be lazy in youth. Otherwise，it will be too late to regret in old age.

Ex. 甲：读书真辛苦。我真想趁年轻的时候好好儿玩玩。

乙：别忘了，少壮不努力，老大徒伤悲。你现在正是学知识、长本领的时候。

甲：那您年轻的时候不是也喜欢旅游吗？

乙：玩是玩，但不能误了正事。

Quot. 百川东到海，何时复西归？少壮不努力，老大徒伤悲。（《乐府诗集·长歌行》）

Cf. 黑发不知勤学早，白首方悔读书迟/桃花年年花相似，人人年年不相同/时间好像东流水，奔流到海不复回

Var. 少小不努力，老大徒伤悲/少小不勤学，老大徒伤悲

He who does not learn when he is young will regret it when he is old

【义】年少不学习，年老时就会后悔。

【解】人们应该趁年轻精力旺盛的时候抓紧学习，否则就会错过大好时光，到老年时就会后悔。

【例】A：It's so boring to study every day. I really want to have time to enjoy my life when I'm young.

B：Don't forget that **he who does not learn when he is young will regret it when he is old**.

A：Easier said than done. You went sight-seeing a lot when you were young, didn't you?

【参】Learning is better than house and land. / There is no royal road to learning. / It's never too late to learn. / If you lie upon roses when young, you'll lie upon thorns when old.

Shībài shì chénggōng zhī mǔ

失败是成功之母

Voc. 失败 failure，成功 success，之 of，母 mother

Lit. Failure is the mother of success.

Exp. Don't give up due to a failure. You'll succeed if you keep learning and trying after the failure.

Ex. 甲：你今年还参加学校的乒乓球比赛吗？

乙：唉，算了吧。连着三年都没拿到名次。

甲：别灰心嘛！失败是成功之母，有了前几次的经验，这次说不定就能赢呢！

Quot. 越是没有经验，越要大胆试验。大胆的试验，是成功的一半。俗话说，失败是成功之母嘛！（郭澄清《大刀记》）

Cf. 吃一堑，长一智/在哪儿跌倒就在哪儿爬起来

Var. 失败乃成功之母/失败者成功之母/失败为成功之母

Failure teaches success

【义】失败是成功之师。

【解】只有不怕失败，从失败中吸取经验，才能最终成功。

【例】A：When was the last time you submitted your application to the university? I think the deadline is coming up soon, isn't it?

B：Yes. The deadline is the day after tomorrow. It has been a while since my application was rejected last time. I'm getting frustrated.

A：You should keep trying. **Failure teaches success**, you know.

B：I know. I shouldn't get so discouraged. I'll turn in my application again, and I'll improve my test score at the same time. If I keep trying, I am sure to succeed eventually.

【引】It is an old . . . saying that failure is the only high-road to success. (G. Balfour, *Life of Stevenson I.* , 1902)

【参】Second trial often succeed. / Succeed or die trying. / The first pancake is always a flop. (Russian) / The good artist is a successful failure. / If at first you don't succeed, try, try again. / If at first you don't succeed, keep on sucking till you do succeed.

【异】Failure is the mother of success. / Three failures and a fire make a Scotsman's fortune.

Shí ge zhǐtou bù yìbān qí

十个指头不一般齐

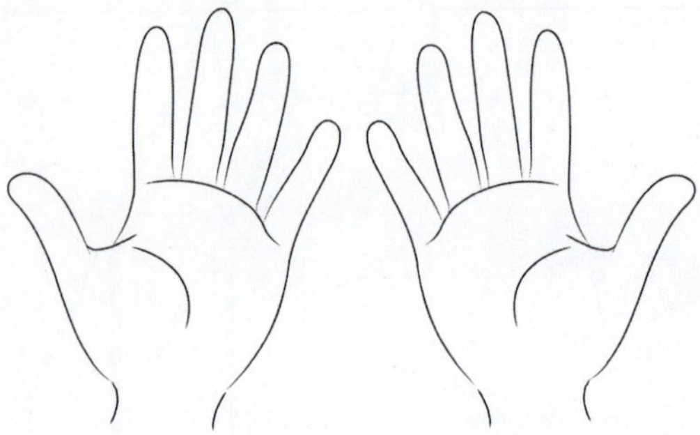

Voc. 指头 finger，一般 same，齐 even

Lit. The ten fingers are not of equal length.

Exp. Every group of people has some members who are different from others. Don't expect everybody or everything to be the same.

Ex. 甲：我真不明白他为什么逃学跟小流氓在一起。你知道，他的哥哥姐姐都是班里的好学生，他的父母也都非常和善厚道。

乙：没什么奇怪的，十个指头不一般齐。

甲：不错。不能指望每个家庭的成员都是一样的。但是，我希望他至少受到家庭的一些正面影响。

Quot. 黄豆里边也掺着黑豆，十个指头不一般齐。俺家也有在都市搞地下工作的……（李英儒《野火春风斗古城》）

Cf. 一树之果，有酸有甜/一母之子，有愚有贤/树大有枯枝/瓜无滚圆，人无十全

Var. 五个指头，总有长短/十个指头有长短/十个手指有长短

There is a black sheep in every flock

【义】每个羊群中都会有一只黑羊。（注：黑羊与白羊相比，通常被看做是劣等的，因为他们的毛难以染色。）

【解】比喻在任何家庭或团体都难免有个别的人或坏人，不要指望大家都一样。

【例】A：I can't understand why he quits school to hang around with bad guys. Both his sister and brother, you know, are top students in their classes. His parents are also very nice and kind.

B：I guess **there's a black sheep in every flock**.

A：That's true. We shouldn't expect that everyone in a family will be the same. However, I wish he could get some good influence from his family at least.

【引】"Nancy is a dreadful woman without a thought in her head," Professor Robinson said years later, "A frozen face. Every family has a black sheep, mine just happens to be famous." (Kitty Kelley, *Nancy Reagan*, 1991)

【参】There is no garden without its weeds.

【异】There is a black sheep in every family. / There are black sheep in every fold.

Shǒuxīn shǒubèi dōu shì ròu

手心手背都是肉

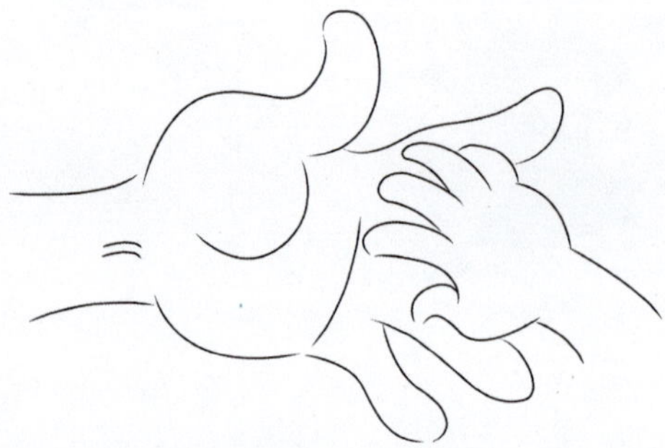

Voc. 手心 center of the palm，手背 back of a hand

Lit. Both the palm and the back of a hand are flesh.

Exp. People of the same family do not destroy one another. Instead, they should be impartial and take care of each other.

Ex. 甲：小强，别欺负你妹妹。
乙：妈妈，她在玩我的电脑。
甲：让她玩玩吧。
乙：你总是偏向妹妹。
甲：胡说！手心手背都是肉，你们俩我都疼。你是哥哥，应该照顾妹妹，兄妹俩应该互相帮助才对呀。

Quot. 这可难坏我了！手心手背都是肉，公公丈夫都是亲人，叫我怎么说啊？（严霞峰《况公案》）

Cf. 是一亲，挂一心/是亲三分向，是火热过炕/是亲有三顾

Var. 手心是肉，手背也是肉/手背是肉，手掌也是肉

Hawks will not pick out hawks' eyes

【义】鹰不会啄鹰的眼睛。

【解】比喻同类不会互相残害。

【例】A：Ted，leave your sister alone.

B：But Mom！She is playing with my computer.

A：That's all right，for your computer is for sharing，besides **hawks will not pick out hawks' eyes**.

B：What are you talking about？What do hawks have to do with my computer？

A：It means those from the same family support and help each other，for example，sharing their computers，rather than being cruel and uncaring.

【引】I have heard that hawks should not pick out hawks' eyes. What do you propose to gain？（J. Buchan，*Salute to Adventures*）

【参】Dogs will not eat dogs. / Dog doesn't eat dog.

【异】Crows will not pick out crows' eyes.

Shù zhèng bú pà yuè yǐng xié

树正不怕月影斜

Voc. 影 shadow，斜 crooked

Lit. A straight tree is not afraid of its crooked shadow.

Exp. One won't fear gossip and others as long as he is doing the right thing.

Ex. 甲：我想买点儿东西送给我们班的同学小李。他是从农村来的，生活挺困难。

乙：好啊。同学之间应该互相帮助嘛。

甲：但是我怕别的同学说闲话。

乙：没关系，树正不怕月影斜。只要你认为自己做得对，就去做吧。

Quot. 虎崽嘟囔道："巡视员知道了，又要说石亮同志进行宗派活动了。"石亮笑起来说："这个我倒不怕，树正不怕月影斜嘛。"（罗旋《南国烽烟》）

Cf. 心正不怕邪，路正不怕蛇/脚正不怕鞋歪/人正不怕影子歪

Var. 树正不怕影子斜/根深不怕风摇动，树正不愁月影斜

Do right and fear no man

【义】做得对就谁也不怕。

【解】意指凡事只要行得正，做得对，就会心中无鬼，敢做敢当。

【例】A：Bill, you had better tell Mr. Smith you broke his window.
B：I know I should, but I am afraid he will be angry.
A：Bill, **do right and fear no man.**
B：What do you mean?
A：I mean if you tell Mr. Smith the truth, he'll appreciate your honesty and you will know you've done the right thing, and you won't have to worry all the time whether or not he knows it was you.

【引】It used to be, "Do right and fear no man. Don't write and fear no women." (Mar, *Guardian*)

【参】An upright man fears no gossip. / Do what is right, come what may. / Do wrong once and you'll never hear the end of it.

【异】Do well and doubt no man.

Shuǐ cóng yuánliú shù cóng gēn

水从源流树从根

Voc. 源流 source and course (of a river, etc.), 根 root

Lit. Water comes from the source and a tree grows up from the root.

Exp. Everything has its source and course.

Ex. 甲：昨晚的音乐会你觉得怎么样？

乙：没想到，那个年轻的吹萨克斯管的真不简单！

甲：是呀，他太棒了！可能因为他的爸爸也是一个著名的萨克斯管演奏家吧。水从源流树从根嘛。

乙：你说得有道理。孩子往往继承他们父母的天才。那个年轻人真是有福气，生活在音乐之家，从小就受到音乐的熏陶。

Quot. 水从源流树从根。这厮既然有投邓车之说，还须上邓家堡去找寻。（《三侠五义》，第六十六回）

Cf. 龙生龙，凤生凤，老鼠生儿会打洞/龙生龙子，虎生豹儿

Var. 水有源，病有根/水有源，树有根

The apple doesn't fall far from the tree

【义】苹果落地，离树不远。

【解】比喻孩子跟父母在相貌、体格、性格、才能等方面往往很相像。

【例】A：What did you think of last night's concert?

B：Wasn't that something? That young saxophone player was incredible!

A：I know! He was amazing. I guess his father was also a famous saxophone player. **The apple doesn't fall far from the tree**.

B：You've got that right. Children usually carry on the traits of their parents. That saxophone player is lucky to have been raised by one of the best musicians in the world. It certainly influenced him.

【引】The apple doesn't fall far from the tree. Geographically that's still true in many American families — popular perceptions notwithstanding. (*Modern Maturity*)

【参】It runs in the family. / Like father, like son. / Like mother, like daughter.

Shuō yì chǐ bùrú xíng yí cùn

说一尺不如行一寸

Voc. 尺 traditional unit of length，行 walk，寸 traditional unit of length（1 尺 =10 寸）

Lit. One foot of speaking is shorter than one inch of walking.

Exp. Taking actions is more convincing than speaking.

Ex. 甲：今天真让我生气！

乙：怎么啦？

甲：我请我哥哥来帮我刷房。他说完全没问题，可是他根本没来。

乙：你知道，说一尺不如行一寸。

甲：是啊。了解一个人不光要听他怎么说，更要看他怎么做。

Quot. 语云："说一尺不如行一寸。"学者尝令精神在内，即有所见，且反躬体贴去，无遽行之言说，正是学问进步处。（刘宗周《证人社约》）

Cf. 光说不行，做出再看/说到做到，不放空炮/说一千，道一万，二横一竖就靠干/说千道万，不如一干/光说不练假把式

Var. 说得一丈，不如行取一尺；说得一尺，不如行取一寸

Actions speak louder than words

【义】行动比言语更响亮。

【解】每个人所做的比他所说的更有说服力。

【例】A：I am a little upset.

B：Why is that?

A：I asked my brother to come over today to help me paint the house. He said he would come, but he didn't show up.

B：Well, you know, **actions speak louder than words**.

A：Yes, I know people's actions reveal more about what they think or feel than what they say.

【引】Actions speak louder than words. Perhaps the first thing parents should consider when their child lies is how prone they are to lying themselves. (*Reader's Digest*, 1991)

【参】Easier said than done. /Deeds, not words.

Sǐ jiāolóng bùrú huó lǎoshǔ

死蛟龙不如活老鼠

Voc. 蛟龙 flood dragon，老鼠 rat

Lit. A dead flood dragon isn't as good as a living rat.

Exp. It's better to be alive and vigorous than to be lifeless and stagnant. It suggests it is better sometimes to give up to those in authority than to fight against them and be ruined.

Ex. 甲：你的旅行怎么样？假期过得好吗？

乙：别提了。旅游点景色不错，但是我们不得不提前结束旅行，因为我们在那里的第二天晚上被五个坏蛋抢劫了。他们抢走了我们所有的钱，结果只好请父母电汇，我们才有钱回家。

甲：真糟糕。我以为你会武术，你怎么不给他们点颜色看看？

乙：会是会。可是一个人跟五个打，疯啦？幸亏我没去冒险。我师傅常说，死蛟龙不如活老鼠。我不在乎别人以为我胆小，有些事不值得拿性命冒险。

Quot. 谚云：“死蛟龙不若活老鼠。”可悟作诗文之旨。（清 · 袁枚《随园诗话 · 补遗》）

Cf. 好死不如赖活/得缩头时且缩头，去时凤凰不如鸡/好死不如歹活

Var. 死蛟龙不若活老鼠

Better a live dog than a dead lion

【义】一个死了的狮子不如一条活着的狗。

【解】表示如果能保存实力，以待今后，比凭一时的硬打死拼要明智，效果好。

【例】A：How was your trip? Did you have a nice vacation?

B：Not really. The scenery was very nice but we had to cut our trip short. We got mugged at the second night there by five guys. They took all of our money and we had to wire my parents for money just to get home.

A：That's terrible. I thought you knew *kungfu*. Why didn't you do something?

B：I know *kungfu*, but against five guys, are you crazy? I was happy just to be alive. My master always says, "**Better a live dog than a dead lion.**" I don't care if anyone thinks I was afraid to fight or not. Some things are not worth risking your life.

【引】... there was nothing better for me to do than to escape speedily into the land of the Philistines if I did not wish to perish one day by the hand of Saul. A living dog is better than a dead lion. (Joseph Heller, *God Knows*)

【参】Better bend than break. / Discretion is the better part of valor. / Better a live coward than a dead hero. / He who fights and runs away, may live to fight another day.

【异】A living dog is better than a dead lion.

Tiānshang méi xià qián, dìli méiyǒu bǎo

天上没下钱，地里没有宝

Voc. 下 come down / fall，宝 treasure

Lit. Money doesn't fall from the heaven and treasures don't come out from the earth.

Exp. If you want to have something, you must work for it and earn it.

Ex. 甲：妈妈，这个周五有舞会，我得穿一身新衣服。

乙：你为什么不穿那件红的呢？

甲：上次舞会我已经穿过了。你可以给我钱去买身新的吗？

乙：又找我要钱？如果你非要买，就用自己的钱。

甲：可是我的钱都花完了。

乙：天上没下钱，地里没有宝。你花钱要仔细点儿，而且必须学会靠自己的劳动去赚钱才行。

Quot. 劳动，治好了他的懒病；勤劳，给他带来了幸福。正如民间谚语所说："天上没下钱，地里没有宝……"（一虹《对劳动的赞颂》）

Cf. 天上不会掉馅饼/樱桃好吃树难栽/出多少汗，吃多少饭/天落馒头，也要起早去拾

Money does not grow on trees

【义】钱不会从树上长出来。

【解】赚钱需要付出劳动与艰辛。泛指一切收获都来之不易。

【例】A：Dad, I need to have a new dress for the dance this Friday.

B：Why don't you wear the red one that you bought last month?

A：I already wore that to the last dance. I couldn't possibly wear it again. I need a new one. Can I have some money to get a new dress?

B：Why do you need my money? Use your own money if you want to buy a new dress.

A：But Dad! I spent all my money. Can I have some, please?

B：**Money does not grow on trees**. You need to be more responsible with your money. You must work for it and earn it.

【引】"Money doesn't grow on trees," she would often say, using the ancient cliché, then add, "in fact, it doesn't grow anywhere unless you plant it, water it and cultivate it." (*Times*)

【参】There is no pleasure without pain. / Nothing seek, nothing find. / If you wait upon fortune, you'll never be sure of your dinner.

【异】Jobs don't grow on trees. / Happiness doesn't grow on trees.

Tiānshang xià yǔ dìshang huá, gèzì diēdǎo gèzì pá

天上下雨地上滑，各自跌倒各自爬

Voc. 滑 slippery，跌倒 fall，爬 clamber

Lit. The road is slippery when it is raining; you have to clamber up by yourself if you fall.

Exp. It suggests that people should rely on themselves to overcome difficulties or correct mistakes.

Ex. 甲：快点儿复习吧，明天你要去补考。
乙：妈妈，我想等哥哥给我辅导一下再说。
甲：别忘了，天上下雨地上滑，各自跌倒各自爬。
乙：您的意思是我应该自己复习？
甲：当然啦。你上次考试不及格，现在你必须靠自己的努力去弥补。快复习吧！

Quot. 他把手放在杨亮的肩头上，朗朗地说："你说得对！天上下雨地上滑，各自跌倒各自爬，要翻身得靠自己。"（丁玲《太阳照在桑干河上》）

Cf. 靠天靠地，不如靠自己/自己的梦自己圆

Var. 自己跌倒自己爬，谁也不能把谁拉/自己跌倒自己爬

God helps those that help themselves

【义】自助者天助。

【解】比喻凡事最好靠自己去努力。

【例】A：Get up, Mike, go to class!

B：Tiffany, I don't want to go! It is too difficult for me.

A：Remember：**God helps those that help themselves.**

B：I think you are mean for waking me up.

A：Maybe so, but you have to go to class and do your work yourself because God won't pass your class for you. Now, get up!

【引】This is the truth：You are a hick and nobody ever helped a hick but the hick himself. Up there in town they won't help you. It is up to you and God, and God helps those who help themselves! (Robert penn Warren, *All the King's Men*)

【异】God helps him who helps himself. / God helps them who help themselves. / The Lord helps those who help themselves.

Wánhuǒzhě bì zìfén

玩火者必自焚

Voc. 玩火 play with fire，者 one or those who，自焚 burn oneself to death

Lit. Whoever plays with fire will perish by it.

Exp. It warns those who are aggressive will eat their own bitter fruit.

Ex. 甲：真是恶人先告状。这个人明明做了坏事，却把受害人告上了法庭。

乙：玩火者必自焚。一切都要根据事实说话。

甲：是啊。我相信事实总会搞清楚的。

Quot. 火是敌人点起的，玩火者自焚，革命的怒火，将会把历史的垃圾烧个干净。(陆地《瀑布》)

Cf. 多行不义必自毙/自己掘坑自己埋/种瓜得瓜，种豆得豆，谁种下仇恨谁自己遭殃

Var. 玩火自焚/玩火者自焚/披麻救火，惹焰烧身

If you play with fire, you get burnt

【义】如果你玩火就会烧到自身。

【解】比喻挑起事端的人往往自食其果。

【例】A：Did you hear the news? Bill was shot the other day.

B：I'm not surprised.

A：How can you not be surprised? Bill is our friend! He might die.

B：**If you play with fire, you get burnt.**

A：What's that supposed to mean?

B：Bill was always getting into fights. He was always provoking other people and he became angry so often. It's not surprising that he made someone angry enough to shoot him. When a person treats others like that, he can expect them to treat him the same way.

【引】If people will play with fire, they must expect to be burned by it some time. If I had not learned the game, and thought myself a good player, I'd never have lost Mother's money. (R. H. Thorpe, *Fenton Family xiv.*)

【参】He who lives by the sword dies by the sword. / If you want peace, prepare for war. / Fight fire with fire. / He who digs a pit for others, falls in himself.

【异】He that touches pitch shall be defiled.

Wànshì kāitóu nán

万事开头难

Voc. 万 ten thousand，开头 beginning

Lit. Everything is hard in the beginning.

Exp. The most difficult part of any undertaking is the beginning step.

Ex. 甲：最近在忙什么？
乙：我正在准备行李，到美国去留学。
甲：离家那么远，你紧张吗？
乙：的确有点儿紧张。这是我第一次出国。
甲：万事开头难。刚开始困难肯定很多，但是到那儿生活一段时间后你就会适应了。
乙：希望如此。

Quot. 万事开头难，今年是大建设的头一年，一切都在忙忙乱乱中摸索，何况又是白手起家。（杜鹏程《光辉的里程》）

Cf. 好的开始，就是成功的一半/头三脚难踢，开锣的戏难唱

Var. 万事起头难/凡事起头难

It's the first step that is difficult

【义】第一步最难走。

【解】比喻事情开始的时候最难办，因而也最重要，要有克服困难的准备。

【例】A：Hi, Kyle! How are you?

B：Hello, Mary. I am packing to go to college in California.

A：Boy, that is a long way away from Michigan. Are you nervous?

B：I am nervous. It is my first time away from home, family and friends.

A：**It is the first step that is difficult**. Remember moving out there will be challenging, but once you've been there a while, you will be more comfortable. Have a safe trip.

B：Thanks for your advice, Mary.

【引】The wise man said, "The distance ... is not important. It was the first step that was difficult." (J. Barnett, *Backfire Is Hostile*)

"Let go," he urges his son. "You can do it, the first step is the hardest, the second will be easier." (*Family Circle*, 1992)

【参】A journey of a thousand miles begins with one step. / The first one hundred years are the hardest. / There must be a first time for everything. / The first essential of a typist is a good eraser.

【异】The first step is the hardest. / It's the first step that counts. / It's the first step that costs. / The first mile is always the hardest.

Wú fēng bù qǐ làng

无风不起浪

Voc. 无 there is not，浪 wave

Lit. No waves if no wind.

Exp. There must be a cause or a reason behind every event or incident (it often refers to an unpleasant incident).

Ex. 甲：跟我们合作的那家公司要倒闭了，你知道吗？

乙：为什么？

甲：听说公司老板贪污了公款。

乙：有证据吗？

甲：还没有，但正在查账。俗话说，无风不起浪，我们还是小心点儿吧。

Quot. 无风不起浪，要是没有一点影子，社员绝对不会这样议论你。（浩然《艳阳天》）

Cf. 无风树不动，要动就是风/无云不下雨/无风树不摇，没缝蛆不生/风不来，树不动；船不摇，水不浑/无潮水自平/事有因，话有缘

Var. 没风不起浪/无风不起浪，没柴不冒烟/无风不起浪，无根不长草/无风不起浪，无鱼水不浑

Where there's smoke, there's fire

【义】冒烟的地方一定有火。

【解】比喻任何事情的发生都有原因。

【例】A: Hey, Mary, why are you still riding your bicycle? I thought you were buying a car yesterday.

B: Well, I planned on buying a used car from the dealership down the road. The trouble is, after I took the car out for a short test drive I noticed it was leaking some dark fluid from somewhere underneath. The dealer said it was just a little oil and it wasn't anything significant.

A: But you still didn't buy it, did you?

B: No, I looked over to where the car had been parked and there were all sorts of huge stains on the ground. I thought to myself, "**Where there's smoke, there's fire**." Maybe the car did only have a small leak, but from what I'd seen, I suspected otherwise. The presence of the oil indicated that there were probably bigger problems ahead.

【引】"Do you have proof of this?" "No," the computer replied, "but where there's smoke, there's fire." (Art Buchwald, *Washington Is Leaking*, 1976)

【参】You can hide the fire, but not the smoke. / Love and smoke cannot be hidden. / When the river runs, it brings water. (Spanish)

【异】If there's smoke, there is fire. / No smoke without a fire. / There's no smoke without fire. / Where there's smoke, there's campaign.

Wù yǐ lèi jù, rén yǐ qún fēn

物以类聚，人以群分

Voc. 物 things，以 according to ，类 type，聚 get together，群 group，分 divide

Lit. Things of a kind come together, and people of a mind fall into the same group.

Exp. People with same interests or characters tend to associate with each other and stay together. It is often used in a negative sense to point out the collaboration of bad elements.

Ex. 甲：你知道约翰在哪儿吗？怎么不管我什么时候回家，他都不在？

乙：他整天跟他的朋友混在一起，半夜三更才回来。你还不懂嘛，物以类聚，人以群分呀。

甲：是啊，脾气或兴趣相投的人往往喜欢在一起。但是，我希望那些跟他在一起的朋友都不是坏人。

乙：我也希望这样。我们可能需要了解一下儿他到底对什么感兴趣。

Quot. 方以类聚，物以群分。（《易·系辞上》）

如藤倚树，物以类聚。（《五灯会元·天衣聪禅师》）

Cf. 鱼找鱼，虾找虾，乌龟找王八/穷找穷亲，富找富邻/凤有凤巢，鸡有鸡窝/烂肉招苍蝇，物聚于所好

Var. 方以类聚，物以群分/物以类聚/人以类聚，物以群分

Birds of a feather flock together

【义】羽毛相同的鸟成群聚集在一起。(flock，聚集)

【解】比喻性格、类型相同的人往往关系密切。有时带有贬义。

【例】A：Do you know where John is? Whenever I come home, he has gone.

B：I guess he has been hanging around with his friends. He always goes out as soon as he gets back home, and he won't be back until midnight. As you know, **birds of a feather flock together**.

A：That's right. People with the same interests usually intend to associate with each other and stay together. However, I hope his friends are nice guys.

B：I hope so, too. Maybe we need to know more about what he has been doing, then we might be able to share his interests.

【引】Birds of a feather flock together, and in our village the few feckless ... tended to live at one end; the prim ... and prosperous at the other. (W. Foley, *Child in Forest*, 1974)

Who are the guys that mostly asked to the clubs? Preppies from St. Paul's, Mark's, Groton. It's kind of common bond. You know, birds of a feather flocking together and so forth. (Erich Segal, *The Class*, 1985)

【参】A man is known by the company he keeps. / As a man is, so is his company. / Tell me what company you keep, and I'll tell you what you are. (Spanish)

【异】Birds of a feather will fly together. / Birds of a feather laugh together. / Birds of a feather gather no moss. / Birds of a feather are drawn together.

Xiān xiàshǒu wéi qiáng

先下手为强

Voc. 先下手 strike first，强 prevail

Lit. He who strikes first prevails.

Exp. Whoever takes action early or first has a better chance of success.

Ex. 甲：春节快到了，我想回老家看看。

乙：你订好飞机票了吗？

甲：还没有。着什么急呀？

乙：你难道不知道春节期间飞机票很紧张？先下手为强，不然买不到票你就“遭殃”了。

Quot. 万一他们来炸城，那我们就完了。所以，我想先下手为强，出其不意，一网打尽。（郭沫若《郑成功》）

Cf. 捷足先登/先下米先吃饭

Var. 先下手为强，后下手遭殃

The early bird catches the worm

【义】早起的鸟才能抓到虫子。

【解】表示凡事应该赶早不赶晚，早行动往往有更多更好的机会。同时也用于劝告人别睡懒觉。

【例】A：Are you going to watch the NBA final at LA?

B：I really want to do that. However, the tickets have already sold out. Do you have one?

A：Yes. I ordered it two months ago.

B：I should remember that **the early bird catches the worm**, since the worm is up early.

【引】The early birds get the worm and the early and late fisherman or woman who offers the worm in the right way will get more fish. (*Times*, 1993)

【参】First come, first served.

【异】It is the early bird that catches the worm. / The early birds are getting all the worms.

Xīnjí chī bu liǎo rè dòufu

心急吃不了热豆腐

Voc. 急 impatient，豆腐 *tofu* (bean curd)

Lit. You can't eat hot *tofu* without patience.

Exp. It tells us to be patient — the greater our need for haste, the more likely we are to waste time.

Ex. 甲：你怎么总是慌慌张张的？慢一点儿！坐下来和我聊聊天儿，怎么样？

乙：不行，不行，我这个星期忙死了。明天的大会发言我还没准备呢。

甲：别忘了，心急吃不了热豆腐。

乙：什么？

甲：记住，事情越多，越要冷静。不然，是做不成事的。

Quot. 老桑料得远，心急吃不了热豆腐，我差一点儿干冒失了。（丁仁堂《渔》）

Cf. 欲速则不达/心急绣不出好花/心急吃不得热汤圆/心慌不能热粥，跑马不能看三国/心急吃不了焖火饭，嘴急喝不上豆儿粥

More haste, less speed

【义】过急反迟。

【解】表示办事情要有充分准备，按部就班地进行，否则，往往会适得其反。

【例】A：Samuel, you are always in a hurry — slow down! Why don't you have a cup of coffee with me?

B：Sorry, I am busy this week, Grandma. I have a meeting tomorrow and a presentation due on Friday.

A：Just remember：**More haste, less speed**.

B：What do you mean? I don't have time for games.

A：That's exactly what I mean. Slow down, the faster you go the more mistakes you will make in your meeting and your presentation.

【引】It snaps because you're in a hurry. You get so flustered that you pull too hard on it, which makes you later than ever. More haste, less speed. (R. Ridout & C. Witting, *English Proverbs Explained*, 1967)

【参】Haste makes waste. / Haste not, waste not. / Haste makes waste, waste makes want, want makes beggars. / Slow and steady wins the race. / Easy does it.

Xīnhūn bùrú yuǎn bié

新婚不如远别

Voc. 婚 marriage，别 leave each other

Lit. A new marriage is less affectionate than a far and long separation.

Exp. A couple often feel more affectionate toward each other when they are apart.

Ex. 甲：你好像很难过，怎么啦？

乙：我想我的女朋友。我已经一年没见到她了。我觉得一天比一天更爱她了。

甲：是啊。新婚不如远别。在一起的时候，我们往往不在意，但是分别以后，我们才感到对方对我们是多么重要。

乙：我保证我的女朋友回来后我一定带她去度个长假。

Quot. 庆贺放赏已毕，贾琏仍复搬进卧室。见了凤姐，正是俗语云"新婚不如远别"，更有无限恩爱。(曹雪芹《红楼梦》，第二十一回)

Var. 新婚不如久别/新婚不如远隔/久别当新婚/小别胜新婚

Absence makes the heart grow fonder

【义】分别会使心中增添情感。

【解】当人们分别以后往往才更多地感受到相互间的感情。(注：包括友情和爱情)

【例】A：Phil, why are you so sad?

B：I miss my girlfriend. I haven't seen her in one year. I realize I love her more and more with each passing day.

A：Yes, **absence makes the heart grow fonder**. When a person is with us, we tend to take him for granted. But when he is away from us, we realize how important he is to us.

B：I promise you that I will take her for a long vacation when she is back.

【引】"I'm not as naïve as I used to be, to believe that absence makes the heart grow fonder," she once wrote bitterly to her faraway husband. (*New York Times*, 1991)

【异】Absence makes the heart grow younger. / Distance makes the heart grow fonder.

Yǎnjing shì xīnlíng de chuānghu

眼睛是心灵的窗户

Voc. 心灵 heart，窗户 window

Lit. Eyes are the window of the heart.

Exp. We can see what's on a person's mind from the expression in his eyes.

Ex. 甲：她生你的气了，是吗？
乙：你怎么知道？
甲：看她的眼睛。常言说，眼睛是心灵的窗户。
乙：什么意思？
甲：一个人的眼睛往往反映出他内心的思想和感情。难道你没看见，她狠狠地瞪了你一眼吗？

Quot. 俗话说，眼睛是心灵的窗户，只要看一下他的那对眼睛，就能猜透他的心思。（张俊彪《山鬼》）

Cf. 眼是观光珠，嘴是试金石/眼是五官门，耳是七窍窗

Var. 眼为心之窗/眼睛是心灵的镜子

The eyes are the window of the soul

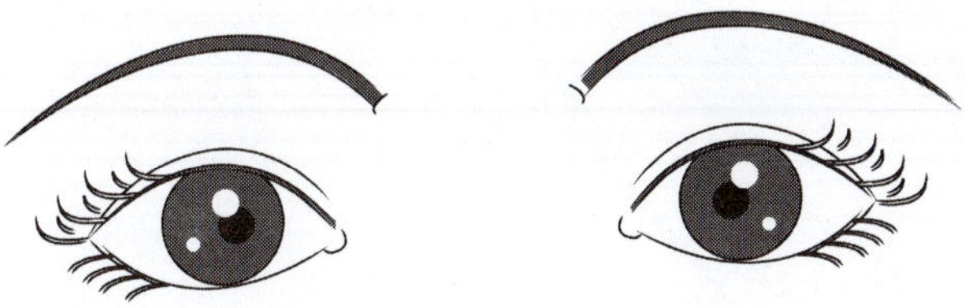

【义】眼睛是灵魂的窗户。

【解】比喻从人的眼睛里往往可以看到这个人的内心和思想活动，所以眼睛是不会说谎的。

【例】A：Boy，is she angry with you?

B：How could you tell?

A：By her eyes. Have you heard the expression **the eyes are the window of the soul**?

B：No，what does it mean exactly?

A：It means a person's eyes reveal their inner thoughts and feelings. It looked like her eyes were throwing darts at you，so I realized that she was angry.

【引】The eyes are said to be the mirror of the soul，but with a new special effect used in "The Shadow"，the eyes (covered with Mylar contact lenses) can also mirror the lighting ... (*New York Times*，1994)

【异】The eyes are the mirror of the soul (mind).

Yǎo rén de gǒu bú jiào, wāngwāng jiào de gǒu bù yǎo rén

咬人的狗不叫，汪汪叫的狗不咬人

Voc. 咬 bite，叫 bark（bowwow）

Lit. Biting dogs do not bark, and barking dogs do not bite.

Exp. It means that a man who threatens in a loud voice may not be dangerous; On the contrary, a man who keeps quiet may take real actions.

Ex. 甲：你见过小李的男朋友吗？

乙：没有。他怎么样？

甲：看起来他特别喜欢吹自己。昨晚在咖啡店，他一直在吹嘘自己是了不起的拳击手，谁都打不过他。

乙：常言道，咬人的狗不叫，汪汪叫的狗不咬人。他在吹牛吧？

甲：十有八九是这样。

Quot. 俗话说："咬人的狗不叫，汪汪叫的狗不咬人。"我要是真想溜走，还会事先向班长挂号？（从维熙《风泪眼》）

Cf. 叫唤的猪不抓老鼠/开水不响，响水不开/干打雷不下雨/雷声大，雨点小

Var. 咬人的狗不露齿/咬人的狗不叫，吃羊的狼不闹/咬人的狗暗下口

Barking dogs seldom bite

【义】叫得凶的狗很少咬人。

【解】比喻喜欢声张的人不一定真有行动，而不声不响的人往往有实际的行动。

【例】A：Have you met Jeannine's new boyfriend?

B：No, I haven't. What is he like?

A：Well, he seems to like talking about himself a great deal. Last night at the cafe he kept on talking about what a great fighter he is and about how he could beat up anyone.

B：I've known a few guys like that, but I've also found that **barking dogs seldom bite**.

A：That's exactly what I was thinking too. Most likely it's just an act. He sounds like a braggart. He would like everyone to think he's something, just like a dog that barks to show everyone how ferocious it is. Usually those are not the dogs that are likely to actually bite you.

【引】You know that barking dogs seldom bite. I've had Mr. Tucker for other classes, so I know that he never stays angry for long. (H. Collis, *101 American English Proverbs*, 1992)

【参】Still waters run deep. / His bark is worse than his bite.

【异】A barking dog never bites. / Barking dogs do not bite. / The loud-barking dog seldom bites. / The dog that barks doesn't bite.

Yào bǔ bùrú shí bǔ

药补不如食补

Voc. 药 medicine，食 food，补 nourish

Lit. Nourishing food is better than tonics.

Exp. It suggests that it would be better for a person's health to eat healthy diet than to depend on tonics.

Ex. 甲：妈，最近我觉得没精神，常常打瞌睡。您看我是不是需要挂个号去看医生？

乙：我看，你除了开始发胖以外，别的都正常。你在学校里每天吃些什么？

甲：咳，想吃什么就吃什么呗。

乙：你听说过“药补不如食补”这句话没有？只要多注意一下每天的饮食，就会保持健康，用不着去看医生。

Quot.“药补不如食补”，虽是人人皆知的常谈，实有至理。（高阳《慈禧前传》）

Cf. 大蒜是个宝，常吃身体好/不吸烟，不喝酒，病魔见了绕道走/饭后喝口汤，强似开药方

An apple a day keeps the doctor away

【义】一天一个苹果，医生不用管我。

【解】如果注意每天的饮食，就可以保持健康。

【例】A：Mom, I don't feel that I have enough energy recently, and I am often very sleepy. Do you think I need to make an appointment with my doctor?

B：It is not a bad idea. However, it seems that everything is normal except that you are gaining weight. Have you been paying attention to what you eat every day at school?

A：Well, I just eat what I like.

B：Have you heard that **an apple a day keeps the doctor away**? I think if you watch what you eat every day, you will stay healthy and won't ever need to see a doctor.

【引】An apple a day keeps the doctor away, the saying goes, but the Environment Protection Agency has reservations. (*Forbes*, 1985)

【参】A joke a day keeps my doctor away. / The best doctors are Dr. Diet. / An orgasm a day keeps the doctor away.

【异】An onion a day will keep everybody away. / Eat an apple on going to bed, and you'll keep the doctor from earning his bread.

Yě láng yǎng bu chéng jiā gǒu

野狼养不成家狗

Voc. 野 wild，狼 wolf，养 raise，家狗 domestic dog

Lit. A wild wolf can't be raised to be a domestic dog.

Exp. A man with a wicked nature will never change, just as a wild wolf will never be a dog.

Ex. 甲：你见到田强了吗？他刚从少年教养所放出来。

乙：还没有。但是听说他被送上少年犯法庭以前是个小偷。不知他会不会还像以前一样。

甲：但愿不会。但是你听说过"野狼养不成家狗"吗？

乙：是啊，如果一个人从小就学坏了，那么想彻底改变是很难的。希望这次能在他的身上发生奇迹。

Quot. 真是野狼养不成家狗！你要走也行，先把这十几年的饭钱算清了再走。（胡正《汾水长流》）

Cf. 江山易改，本性难移/野鸡长不了凤凰毛/狗改不了吃屎

The leopard cannot change its spots

【义】豹子不能改变身上的花斑。

【解】常比喻本性难移，就像豹子不能改变它与生俱来的花斑一样。

【例】A：Have you met Tom yet? He just got out from juvey.

B：No, I haven't. I heard he was a thief prior to being sent to the Juvenile Court. I wonder if he will continue stealing things as before.

A：I hope not, but have you heard **the leopard cannot change its spots**?

B：Yes, that's true. Just as you can always identify the leopard by its spots no matter how hard it tries to hide itself, so will we eventually be able to see what kind of person Tom is really like after the correction.

【引】He always was a dirty old man ... and the leopard doesn't change its spots. (J. Scott, *Clutch of Vipers*)

【参】You can't make a silk purse out of a sow's ear.

【异】The leopard cannot change his spots. / The leopard does not change its spots. / You can't change a leopard's spots.

Yí ge bāzhang pāi bu xiǎng

一个巴掌拍不响

Voc. 巴掌 palm，拍 clap

Lit. One hand alone cannot clap.

Exp. 1. Certain results are caused by both parties. Therefore, they are both responsible for the successes or failures. The sense is usually that both parties should be responsible for wrong-doings.

2. Certain activities require mutual cooperation to achieve a common goal.

Ex. 甲：昨天你和你先生是不是吵架了？我在隔壁都听见了。

乙：没错。他也太不讲理了，一回家就发脾气。

甲：一个巴掌拍不响，你肯定也有责任。

乙：他不讲理，我当然就不客气啦。

甲：看来，你们俩都得改改脾气。

Quot. 人主之患在莫之应。故曰：一手独拍，虽疾无声。(《韩非子·功名》)

过去的事就甭提了，一个巴掌拍不响，我也有不好的地方。(老舍《红大院》)

Cf. 一个人是死的，两个人是活的/一个跳蚤顶不起被窝/一个指头握不成拳/一只碗不响，半只碗叮当/一人打铁锤不响，两人打铁响叮当/一足不成步，独拍不成声

Var. 一只手拍不响

It takes two to tango

【义】跳探戈舞得两个人。

【解】比喻一个人势单力薄，难以成事。也表示单方面不能形成矛盾冲突。

【例】A：Look, the touch-up paint doesn't match the original color of the wall. You may have to repaint the whole house. It looks just awful!

B：I told you that I was not good at painting walls. Besides, **it takes two to tango**. If you didn't insist on doing this job by ourselves, I shouldn't have run into this trouble. It was just as much your fault as it was mine.

A：Well, maybe so, but it won't do us any good by arguing who's in fault. What we need right now is to decide how to deal with the mess.

B：I think we need to hire a professional painter to do the job.

【引】There are lots of things you can do alone! But, it takes two to tango. (Hoffman & Manning, *Takes Two to Tango*, *song title*, 1952)

【参】It takes two to make a bargain. / It takes two to make a quarrel. / It takes two to make peace. / It takes two blows to make a battle.

Yí ge xífu shí ge pó

一个媳妇十个婆

Voc. 媳妇 daughter-in-law，婆 mother-in-law

Lit. One daughter-in-law with her ten mothers-in-law

Exp. It won't be good if there are too many people in charge but few people doing the real job.

Ex. 甲：你的新工作怎么样？

乙：老实说，我不知该怎么做。我现在得向老板、经理、两个经理助理和好几个管理人员报告工作。

甲：听起来就让人糊涂。到底有多少人在实际的生产线上呢？

乙：只有我和另外一个人。

甲：真是一个媳妇十个婆。不能每个人都是老板，你们真正需要的是更多的工人。

Quot. 梁队长检查完了，告诉我们“行”，现在你们又叫返工！一个媳妇十个婆婆，哪个婆婆说了算？（杜鹏程《在和平的日子里》）

Cf. 僧多粥少，官多兵少/要想日子甜，家无一人闲

Var. 一个媳妇十个婆婆/一个媳妇九个婆

Too many chiefs, not enough Indians

【义】头人太多，印第安人太少。

【解】比喻管事的人太多，而实际做事的人太少，难以办成事。

【例】A：How is your new job going?

B：Well, quite frankly I'm confused. I have a crew boss, a manager, two assistant managers, and several supervisors that I have to report to.

A：That sounds very confusing. How many people are in charge of the actual production process?

B：Just myself and one other guy.

A：**Too many chiefs, not enough Indians**! Everyone cannot be a boss; you definitely need more workers.

【引】Many a business has had its troubles because it was composed of all chiefs and no Indians. (*Business Talk*)

【异】All chiefs and no Indians. / Too many chiefs and not enough braves.

Yíyàng mǐ yǎng bǎi yàng rén

一样米养百样人

Voc. 米 rice，养 raise

Lit. Various kinds of people are fed by the same rice.

Exp. People are different, and we should recognize the differences between them.

Ex. 甲：我有个朋友，他冬天喜欢游泳，夏天却喜欢滑冰，你说怪不怪？

乙：那有什么奇怪的！

甲：可是夏天游泳，冬天滑冰才符合大家的习惯。

乙：一样米养百样人，世界上什么样的人都有。

Quot. 唉，什么笨事都有人做得出来，真是一样米养百样人。（里汗《新绿林传》）

Cf. 八仙过海，各显其能/千里不同风，百里不同俗/鱼有鱼路，虾有虾路/鱼肉青菜，各有所爱/一个将军一个令，一个和尚一本经

It takes all kinds of people to make a world

【义】世界是由各种各样的人组成的。

【解】由于要有各种各样的人才能组成这个世界，所以每个人都有他自身的作用，我们待人处事也要因人而异，宽容大度。

【例】A：Ryan is strange. Did you hear how he eats apples by cutting them into slices?

B：I prefer to eat my apples whole, but **it takes all kinds of people to make a world**.

A：What are you talking about?

B：Ryan has his own way of eating apples that is different from yours or mine. The world is made of all sorts.

【引】We are not all alike. We differ from each other in many ways — physically, mentally and morally. Some of us are good sorts, some of us are bad sorts, and some of us are a bit of each. So we must be charitable and allow everyone the right to exist. (R. Ridout & C. Witting, *English Proverbs Explained*, 1967)

【参】Variety is the spice of life. / Horses for courses. / Live and let live.

【异】It takes all sorts to make a world.

Yíxīn shēng àn guǐ

疑心生暗鬼

Voc. 疑心 suspicion，生 grow，暗 hidden，鬼 ghost

Lit. Suspicions create fantastic fears.

Exp. One shouldn't be too suspicious to trust others.

Ex. 甲：你脸色怎么这么不好？

乙：唉，我和朋友大吵了一架，搞得我心烦意乱。最近我总倒霉，可能是他在背后捣鬼。

甲：难怪你心情不好。可是你要知道，疑心生暗鬼。别太多心了，还是和你的朋友好好儿谈谈。

Quot. ……我没添一点油，加一点醋。巡视员，你不要疑心生暗鬼！（罗旋《南国烽烟》）

Cf. 疑心生暗鬼，过虑损精神/疑心生暗鬼，眼花便中邪/疑心生暗鬼，不听自然无

Var. 疑中生暗鬼/疑鬼就有鬼

He that follows freits, freits will follow him

【义】相信预兆的人，预兆会跟着他走。(freit/omen 征兆，预兆)

【解】比喻客观情况往往会受到个人潜意识的影响。

【例】A：Betty, why are you so sad?

B：George, my sister and I had a fight, I burnt dinner, and now I've lost my favorite necklace. I'm also afraid that I can't pass my math test tomorrow.

A：It sounds like a frustrating day, but, you know, **he that follows freits, freits will follow him**.

B：I don't understand.

A：It is all in how you look at the situation. If you view a situation in a sad or negative light, other circumstances will also be negative. So look on the bright side — we have had a nice talk today.

【引】He that follows freits, freits will follow him. He that notices superstitious observations ... it will fall to him accordingly. (J. Kelly, *Scottish Proverbs*)

【异】Freits (omens) follow those who look to them.

Yǐ yǎn huán yǎn, yǐ yá huán yá
以眼还眼，以牙还牙

Voc. 以 use，还 fight back

Lit. An eye for an eye, and a tooth for a tooth.

Exp. Use the same methods against your opponent that he or she is using against you.

Ex. 甲：我简直不敢相信，那家公司把我的方案都偷走了。
乙：抱怨也没用，你应该以眼还眼，以牙还牙。
甲：你的意思是……
乙：你也可以把他们的促销方式学过来。反正你们的客户多，位置好，一定会打垮他们的。

Quot. 我们的抗战不仅是报仇，以眼还眼，以牙还牙，而且是打击穷兵黩武。（老舍《四世同堂》）

Cf. 以其人之道，还治其人之身/以毒攻毒，以火攻火

Var. 以手还手，以脚还脚/以牙还牙，以血还血

Fight fire with fire

【义】用火来反击火。

【解】比喻用对方使用的方法或手段来攻击对方。

【例】A：I can't believe that company took my idea. Look at all the business it has created for them.

B：Well, don't complain about it. **Fight fire with fire**.

A：You're referring to implementing more of my creative ideas to outdo them and increase my own business?

B：Exactly, your business has many positive aspects like location and demand. Give the other company more competition than they are giving you.

【引】Mr. Rollins implied that the Republicans were just fighting fire with fire — greasing palms already greased by the Democrats. (*Times*, 1993)

Yì fēn gēngyún, yì fēn shōuhuò

一分耕耘，一分收获

Voc. 耕耘 plough and weed，收获 harvest

Lit. Better ploughing and weeding results in better crops.

Exp. It's impossible to gain anything without an effort.

Ex. 甲：现在的生意真不好做。有时候一天一件商品也卖不出去。

乙：要想把买卖做好，你就得做广告，搞推销，同时不断改进产品。一分耕耘，一分收获。

甲：你说得没错。没有努力，就没有收获。不做广告，顾客也不会自己找上门来。

Quot."一分耕耘，一分收获"，花了一点劳动，就会得到相应的成果。（王卿、刘书祥《谚语小词典》）

Cf. 人要勤劳，地要常刨/出多少汗，吃多少饭/三分天才，七分勤劳

Var. 一分勤劳，一分成果/一分功夫，一成货色

You don't get something for nothing

【义】没有付出就不会得到。

【解】表示任何事情都需要付出努力才能实现。

【例】A: It is so hard to do business nowadays. We have been waiting for customers since we opened up our store.

B: You may need to advertise and promote the sale, instead of just waiting. And **you don't get something for nothing**.

A: You are right. Nothing will come out of nothing.

【引】You don't get something for nothing. If you want the lovely things ... you can't have them unless you're prepared to pay for them. (*Guardian*, 1979)

【参】You can't get blood from a stone. / Nothing seek, nothing find. / Nothing will come out of nothing. / Nothing for nothing. / No pains, no gains.

【异】From nothing, nothing is made.

Yì huā bú shì chūn, dú mù bù chéng lín

一花不是春，独木不成林

Voc. 独 single，木 tree，林 forest

Lit. One flower can't make a spring, and one tree can't make a forest.

Exp. In general usage, this proverb emphasizes people must work together, and nothing can be accomplished by a single person.

Ex. 甲：你们班的约翰汉语说得太棒了！

乙：他可以说得上是一个“中国通”了。但“一花不是春，独木不成林”，我希望班上的每一个外国学生汉语说得都跟他一样好。

甲：严师出高徒，有你这样一个好老师，肯定没问题。

Quot. “一木不成林，一花不成春。”打仗靠协力，胜利靠集体。（李英儒《上一代人》）

Cf. 一个跳蚤顶不起被窝/一个拳头打不出一口井/一人难唱一台戏/一个人浑身是铁，也打不了几根钉/一天春风吹不开遍野花/一只大雁飞走带不走冬天，一只燕子飞回带不来春天/孤木不成林，独木不成桥/一个指头握不成拳

Var. 一花独放不是春，百花齐放春满园/一花独秀不是春，万紫千红春满园

One swallow does not make a summer

【义】一燕不成夏。

【解】比喻只凭一个现象往往不能证明什么事情或做出什么结论。

【例】A: It's really warm today. I think spring is around the corner.

B: I hope so. However, it is still in January. Spring won't be here until March. Do you remember Aristotle, a Greek philosopher, said "**One swallow does not make a summer**", nor does one fine day?

A: You are right. I came here from the south one week ago. It's really cold here. I just wish we could change the weather and keep warm every day.

【引】Two Big Macs, please. After all, one swallow does not make a spring lunch. (*Overheard at McDonald's*)

【参】One piece of evidence is not enough to draw conclusions.

【异】One swallow does not make a spring. / One swallow makes not a summer, not even two swallows.

Yì huí shé yǎo jiǎo, shí nián pà cǎi cǎo

一回蛇咬脚，十年怕踩草

Voc. 蛇 snake，咬 bite，脚 foot，踩 step on，草 grass

Lit. Once bitten by a snake, one shies to step on grass for ten years.

Exp. If one has been hit hard by something, he will be afraid of a similar thing or situation for a long time.

Ex. 甲：今天天气真热，我们去游泳吧。

乙：算了吧。上次我学游泳差点儿被淹死，我再也不去了。

甲：这真是"一回蛇咬脚，十年怕踩草"。其实，游泳没什么危险，我可以教你，还保证你安全。

乙：真的？

Quot. 俗话说："一回蛇咬脚，十年怕踩草。"小范一家真是饿怕了，一提没米少面，就不由得担起心来。（期刊）

Cf. 不怕山高，就怕脚软/明知山有虎，偏向虎山行

Var. 一次挨蛇咬，二次不拔草/一朝被蛇咬，十年怕井绳/一朝被蛇咬，十年怕草绳

Once bitten, twice shy

【义】一次被咬，下次胆小。

【解】意指受过一次惊吓或上过一次当，再遇到类似情况就会格外胆怯。

【引】"Mr. Saunders," said the schoolmistress, "we are taking another party of children up to see the sights of London next Saturday. Would you like to help us as you so kindly did last time?"
"I'm sorry , Miss Osborne, but I 'd much rather not," he replied. "Those infernal kids nearly drove me mad. '**Once bitten, twice shy**' is my motto from now on."
(R. Ridout & C. Witting, *English Proverbs Explained*, 1967)

【参】A burnt child dreads the fire. / He who has suffered shipwreck fears to sail upon the sea.

【异】Once bit, twice shy.

Yì kǒu chī bu xià ge pàng héshang

一口吃不下个胖和尚

Voc. 胖 fat，和尚 monk

Lit. No one grows fat on just one mouthful.

Exp. Don't be overconfident to assume work that you can't handle. Do your work step by step.

Ex. 甲：对不起，我能借一下你的制服吗？

乙：为什么？

甲：今天下午，我要去找工作，可是制服还没拿去洗呢！

乙：其实，我看你连吃饭和睡觉的时间都没有。要知道，一口吃不下个胖和尚。

甲：我知道，我也不想超负荷。但是没办法。我不但得按时毕业，而且还需要很多实际工作的经验。最起码的是，我得有钱付账单。

Quot. 你先别慌，也别急，一口吃不下个胖和尚。（程树榛《钢铁巨人》）

Cf. 贪多嚼不烂/吃不了兜着走/一口吃不成胖子/一口吃不出个大胖子/一锄不能挖个井，一口不能吃个饼

Var. 一口吃不下胖子

Don't bite off more than you can chew

【义】贪多嚼不烂。

【解】告诫人们不要因贪多或心急而做自己能力达不到的事。

【例】A：Oh, my God, can I borrow your suit?

B：Why?

A：I have a job interview this afternoon, and I have no time to do my laundry.

B：I have already noticed that. It seems that you don't even have time to eat and sleep. Listen, **don't bite off more than you can chew.**

A：I know that, and I don't want to take more work than I can handle. However, I have to. I need to graduate on time, and I also need a lot of working experience. The bottom line is that I have to pay my bills.

【引】When you took that full-time job I warned you: Don't bite off more than you can chew! (H. Collis, *101 American English Proverbs*, 1992)

"Last year, we bit off more than we could chew," Mr. Clinton said in a moment of clear-eyed candor, "This year, let's work together, step by step, to get something done." (*New York Times*, 1995)

【参】Rome was not built in a day. / little by little and bit by bit / Don't take a step longer than your leg. / He who does too much often does little.

【异】Don't bite off more than you can take.

Yì qiāo wā bu chū ge jǐng

一锹挖不出个井

Voc. 锹 spade，挖 dig，井 well

Lit. One dig by a spade can't make a well.

Exp. Everything takes time and effort. Nothing will be accomplished without patience.

Ex. 甲：历史课老师要求我们每人写篇二十五页的文章，我还从来没写过这么长的，真有点儿着急了。

乙：这要求高是高，但是要紧的是越早开始越好。别等到期末才写，那样的话肯定糟糕。

甲：你的意思是"一锹挖不出个井"，对不对？

乙：当然。一锹挖不出个井来，一天也写不出一篇好文章。做成每件事都需要时间和努力。

Quot. 心急吃不到热粥，一锹挖不出一口井，自己的钥匙没有对准锁眼，不要怪锁开不开。（海笑《春潮》）

Cf. 万丈高楼平地起/一笔画不成龙，一棍打不死熊/一口吃不成胖子/路要一步步地走，饭要一口口地吃

Var. 一镢头掏不成个井/一锄不能挖个井，一口不能吃个饼

Rome wasn't built in a day

【义】罗马非朝夕建成。

【解】比喻做好任何事都需要耐心和持久不断的努力。有时也用做延迟的借口。

【例】A：What do you think of the requirements for our new history class? I've never written a 25-page term paper before. I'm kind of anxious about that assignment, aren't you?

B：No, not really. It will certainly be a challenge though. The important thing about a term paper is that you begin working on it as soon as possible. Don't wait until the last minute or you will definitely be in trouble.

A：It's like the old saying "**Rome wasn't built in a day**", right?

B：Absolutely! It certainly took more than one day to build the city of Rome, and it will certainly take more than one day to create a good term paper. Everything good takes time and effort. That's for sure.

【引】Life is what you make it. Rome wasn't built in a day. (Cheyney, *Trap for Bellamy*)

【参】It's dogged that does it. / little by little and bit by bit / Little strokers fell great oaks. / Dripping wears away the stone.

【异】Rome was not made in one day.

Yì shú sān fēn qiǎo

一熟三分巧

Voc. 熟 practised，巧 skilful

Lit. Skill comes from practice.

Exp. Practice will make skills.

Ex. 甲：怎么样？你还在学弹钢琴吗？

乙：是啊，我还在上钢琴课。钢琴老师告诉我每天至少要有一个小时的基本功练习，特别单调，我真讨厌这种练习。

甲：这种练习可能没意思，但却是必需的。如果练好了，你就能弹各种曲子了。

乙：这我知道。但我真不喜欢这样的练习。

甲：一熟三分巧嘛。练习可能没意思，但是只有反复练习才能做到熟练。离开了练习，你弹钢琴不会有什么进步的。

Quot. 俗话说的“熟能生巧”，舅兄昨日谈了一夜，不但他已嚼出此中意味，并且连寄女也都听会，所以随问随答，毫不费事。（李汝珍《镜花缘》）

Cf. 曲不离口，拳不离手

Var. 熟能生巧

Practice makes perfect

【义】练习才能达到完美。

【解】只有反复练习才能精确地掌握一门知识或技术。

【例】A: Hello! How are things going? Are you still learning how to play the piano?

B: Oh, yes. I'm still taking piano lessons. My teacher told me I have to practice my scales for at least one hour every day. It's so boring though. I really hate practicing scales.

A: Well, practicing scales may be boring but they are necessary. If you learn your scales, you should be able to play anything.

B: Oh, I know. I just never feel like practicing them.

A: Well, **practice makes perfect**. It may not be much fun but you will only achieve perfection through practice. Without practicing, your piano playing will not amount to much.

【引】It is like playing the piano or riding a bicycle. Practice makes perfect. (D. Lessing, *Shikasta*, 1979)

【参】An ounce of practice is worth a pound of precept. / Learn to walk before you run. / All things are difficult before they are easy.

Yì yán xīng bāng

一言兴邦

Voc. 言 speech / word，兴 rise，邦 country

Lit. A single right statement may invigorate a country.

Exp. The words are more powerful than physical power.

Ex. 甲：你去过中国的深圳吗？
乙：去过，那里又漂亮又现代。
甲：可是你知道吗？几十年前，那里还是个小渔村。
乙：怎么会变化这么大呢？
甲：靠的是邓小平的“南巡讲话”。
乙：真是“一言兴邦”啊！

Quot. 金环洞悉关敬陶的全部底细，可以说她操持了关敬陶的命运。在这一言兴邦，一言丧邦的关头，关敬陶听到“我认识他”的回答。（李英儒《野火春风斗古城》）

Cf. 三寸之舌可杀五尺之躯/舌头杀人不用刀/以力服人身服，以理服人心服/一时强弱在于力，千古胜负在于理/打倒莫如说倒/人怕理，马怕鞭，蚊子怕火烟

Var. 一言可以兴邦，一言可以丧邦/一言而兴邦，一言而丧邦

The pen is mightier than the sword

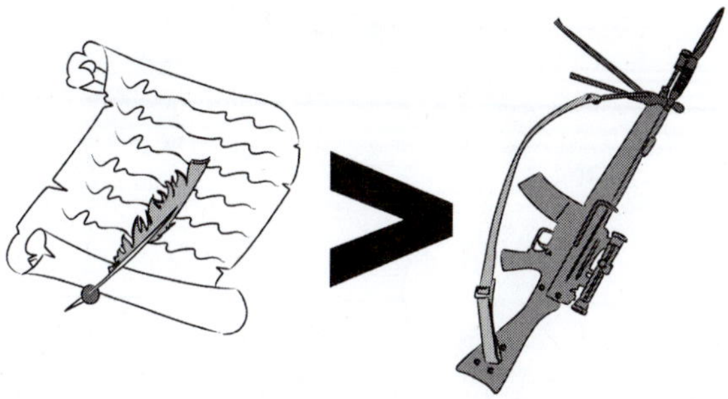

【义】笔比剑更有力。(mighty 有力的，sword 剑)

【解】好的文章比军事力量更有说服力。

【例】A：Have you ever been there?

B：Yes. It's a modern and beautiful city.

A：But do you know it was still a small fishing village a few dozen years ago?

B：Oh, what a great change! Why?

A：A leader made a speech.

B：I see. **The pen is mightier than the sword**.

【引】"It has long been recognized that the pen is mightier than the sword," said Randall L. Tobias, "The modern version of that is: the fax machine is mightier than the rifle." (*New York Times*, 1993)

【参】The pen is the tongue of the mind. / The pen conveys one's meaning a thousand miles. / The pen of the tongue should be dipped in the ink of the heart.

【异】The pen is noisier than the sword. / No more sword to be feared than the learned pen. / The pen is worse than sword.

Yǒu yì dé bì yǒu yì shī

有一得必有一失

Voc. 得 gain，必 must，失 loss

Lit. When there is gain，there is loss.

Exp. We have to accept that it's impossible to succeed or win all the time.

Ex. 甲：你不是在盼提职吗？怎么样？
乙：提了。
甲：祝贺你！这个消息真让人高兴。
乙：谢谢。但是，提了职，工作更忙了。
甲：有一得必有一失。注意休息吧。

Quot. 老张头虽然轻松而又自在……然而却又可能在历史的长河中随波逐流……有得必有失。（《1977 ~ 1980 全国获奖中篇小说集》）

Cf. 有一利必有一弊/智者千虑，必有一失/有一兴必有一败

Var. 有得必有失

You win a few, you lose a few

【义】你赢一些，你也会输一些。

【解】说明一个人不可能任何事都成功。

【例】A：Did you receive the promotion you were expecting at work?

B：Yes, I did.

A：Congratulations! I'm glad to hear that.

B：Thanks. However, **you win a few, you lose a few**. One of my co-workers got mad at me after he found out that I got the promotion.

A：Well, never mind. Although success is nice, we can't always succeed in everything.

B：You are right. I must be ready to accept losses now and again.

【引】You win a few, you lose a few, and it's no good getting sore. (P. O'Donnell, *Sabre-Tooth xiv*, 1966)

It is in his campaigning that you make your mark sometimes you win, sometimes you lose. (Mario Cuomo, *New York Times*, 1994)

【参】You can't win 'em all. / Where there is an advantage, there must be a disadvantage.

【异】You win some, you lose some. / Win some, lose some. / You win one, you lose one.

Yǒu zhì zhě, shì jìng chéng

有志者，事竟成

Voc. 志 will，者 -er，竟 eventually (formal)

Lit. Nothing is impossible to a willing heart.

Exp. Anything is achievable as long as a person is determined.

Ex. 甲：我真想学医，将来当名医生。

乙：那太好啦。但是，你知道医学院很难进吗？就算你考上了，学习时间也很长。那时候你不仅会感到紧张，有压力，而且经济上也非常吃紧。

甲：我明白你的意思。但是，有志者，事竟成。我相信只要下定决心去努力就能实现自己的愿望。

Quot. 我平日相信“有志者，事竟成”的话。你该记得我们从前要进学堂，爷爷起初不是极端反对吗？后来到底是我胜利了。（巴金《家》）

Cf. 天下无难事，只怕有心人/人无志气刀无钢/不怕路远，就怕志短/锲而不舍，金石可镂

Var. 有志者，事竟成；无志者，一切空/有志者自有千方百计，无志者自有千难万难

Where there's a will, there's a way

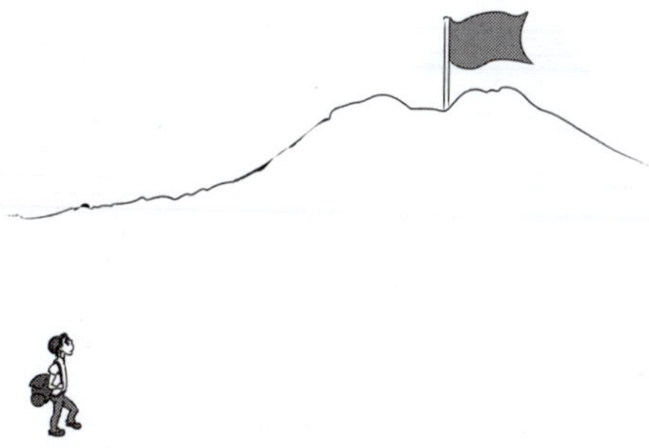

【义】有某种志愿，就有实现这种志愿的道路。

【解】强调只要有意志和决心，就会最终达到自己的愿望。

【例】A：I really want to major in medical science and become a doctor in the future.

B：Good for you! However, have you heard that it is very difficult to get into the medical school? Even if you can make it, it takes a long time to graduate. That means not only will you be stressed, nervous and anxious for almost six years after college, but you will also have to face the financial burden.

A：I understand what you mean. However, **where there's a will, there's a way**. I believe that given sufficient determination, I can accomplish what I set out to do.

【引】I've no idea how it can be done. But where there's a will, there's a way. (E. Koch, *Good Night Little Spy xi*, 1979)

The saying "Where there's a will, there's a way" is not the whole truth. Given the will, you still have to anticipate obstacles and plan how to deal with them. (*Reader's Digest*, 1992)

【参】It's dogged that does it. / Constant dropping wears away a stone. / He who wills the end, wills the means. / If you would be a Pope, you must think of nothing else.

【异】Where there's a will, there are relatives. / Where there's a will, there's a lawsuit. / Where there's a will, there is contestation. / Where there's a will, there's an estate.

Yòu xiǎng chī yángròu, yòu pà rěshang shān

又想吃羊肉，又怕惹上膻

Voc. 惹 cause，膻 smell of mutton

Lit. want to eat mutton, but be afraid of the smell of it

Exp. It's impossible to take the advantages of the two conflicting things at the same time.

Ex. 甲：你最近跟小周谈过吗？不知道他喜不喜欢他的新工作。

乙：昨晚我们刚谈过。他说他的工作还可以，但是对工作的时间不满意，现在他每天六点就得起床。

甲：他总是爱抱怨。你知道，又想吃羊肉，又怕惹上膻是不可能的。

乙：可不是嘛！不可能样样事情都合自己的意。

Quot. 我这个人顶喜欢痛痛快快的，心里想要什么，嘴里就说什么。我可不爱要吃羊肉又怕膻气的男人。（曹禺《曹禺选集》）

Cf. 又想吃大饼，又不愿累牙/又想吃炒豆，又怕炸了锅/又想当婊子，又想立牌坊/又想吃鱼又嫌腥/又想过河，又怕湿鞋/又想好，又想巧，又想老驴不吃草

Var. 想吃羊肉又怕惹上一身腥/要吃羊肉又怕腥气

You can't have your cake and eat it too

【义】你不能又想留着蛋糕，又要吃蛋糕。

【解】比喻想同时得到两个互相矛盾的东西是不可能的。

【例】A：Have you spoken with Joel lately? I wonder how he likes his new job.

B：I spoke with him last night. He said his job was okay, but he was complaining about his work schedule. He has to wake up at 6：00 every morning now.

A：He is always complaining about something! If it wasn't his work schedule, it would be something else. As you know, **you can't have your cake and eat it too**.

B：How true! He should be thankful he has a job. No one gets everything they want in life and no one should expect to have everything they want.

【引】In philosophy and morals the hardest and most essential rule is "You can't eat your cake and have it too", but dialectic overcomes this rule. (Allan Bloom, *The Closing of the American Mind*)

【参】You can't have it both ways.

【异】You can't have everything and eat it too. / Eat your cake and have the crumbs in bed with you. / You can't eat your cake and have it too. / You can't sell the cow and sup the milk.

Yuǎn shuǐ jiù bu liǎo jìn huǒ

远水救不了近火

Voc. 远 far，救火 fight a fire

Lit. Distant water can't put out a fire close at hand.

Exp. It is important to focus on the current situation and the solution rather than those expectations that may be realized too late.

Ex. 甲：我最近在找工作，可总也找不到合适的。
乙：别着急，你肯定能找到好工作的。
甲：我也希望这样。可是，远水救不了近火。你知道吗？我下岗都两个多月了。
乙：又没工作又没钱，日子肯定不好过。要不你随便找个工作先干着。
甲：也只能这样了。

Quot. 巨著的译述，有远水不解近火之苦，最后还是靠私家教课的职务。（邹韬春《经历·深挚的友谊》）

Cf. 远水不解近渴

Var. 远水不及近火/远水救不得近火/远水难救近火

While the grass grows, the steed starves

【义】当草生长的时候，马早已饿死。

【解】马不能等着新草充饥，比喻远不可及的东西不能解决当务之急。

【例】A：What a difficult time! I am waiting to hear back from a job interview.

B：I'm sure you will get the job.

A：I hope so, too. However, **while the grass grows, the steed starves**. You know, I have already been unemployed for two months.

B：It is certainly a predicament to have no money or job. I am sure it is difficult to manage because you can't buy anything without money.

A：It is. Can you treat me to dinner?

【引】I shall sell them next year fast enough, after my one-man show; but while the grass grows the steed starves. (B. Shaw, *Doctor's Dilemma*, 1911)

【异】While the grass grows, the horse lies dying. / While the grass grows, the horse starves.

Zài jiā qiān rì hǎo, chūmén yìshí nán

在家千日好，出门一时难

Voc. 千日 a thousand days，一时 a short while

Lit. When at home，you find life easy and comfortable all the time，and when away from home，you may run into difficulties even for a single day.

Exp. A person is the happiest in his or her own home with his or her family and friends. He or she will have a difficult time whenever he or she is away from home. It is often said when away from home or back home after a tiring time away.

Ex. 甲：你在美国住了多久了？

乙：差不多一年了。

甲：怪不得你都快美国化了。我猜你现在一定习惯美国的生活了吧？

乙：我非常喜欢旅游和旅居国外，当我看到不同的风土人情时总感到快乐。但是我还是特别想念我的老家。再说，在国外谋生也并不容易。在家千日好，出门一时难。你不但会想念家乡的亲人朋友，而且也得为了生活加倍工作才行。

甲：一点儿也不错。一个人觉得最幸福、最舒服的地方总是在他自己的家。

Quot. “没有事找就不找吧，兵荒马乱，出门做什么？自古道：‘在家千日好，出门半时难’！”（李六如《六十年的变迁》）

Cf. 远客归去来，在家贫亦好/坐饮家乡水也甜/穷家难舍，热土难离/金窝银窝，不如自己的穷窝/家穷有口锅，人穷不离窝

Var. 在家千日好，出门刻刻难/在家千日好，出门时时难/在家千日好，出门半朝难

There's no place like home

【义】没有一个地方像家一样。

【解】一个人觉得最幸福和温暖的地方就是在自己的家。

【例】A: How long have you been living in the United States?

B: About one year.

A: No wonder you are so Americanized. I guess you must be used to living in the U. S. now.

B: Well, as you know, I'm very fond of traveling and living abroad, and I always enjoy seeing different people and places. However, I still miss my native land. Living abroad is not easy. Not only do I miss my famliy and friends at home, but I also have to work harder to make a living. **There's no place like home**.

A: That is true. The place a person always feels the happiest and most comfortable is his or her own home.

【引】For some Russian Jews, there's no place like home. (Headline, *Manhattan Jewish Sentinel*, 1994)

【参】Home is where heart is. / Home, sweet home. / Go abroad and you'll hear news of home. / East or west, home's best. / An Englishman's home is his castle. / The longest way round is the shortest way home.

Zhī cuò gǎi cuò bú suàn cuò

知错改错不算错

Voc. 知错 admit it is wrong，算 calculate

Lit. It won't be counted as a mistake, if you can admit it and correct it.

Exp. Don't be afraid of making mistakes. You still have a chance to succeed if you realize your errors and correct them as soon as possible.

Ex. 甲：最近我常常失眠。

乙：为什么？是不是学习压力太大了？

甲：是啊。为了按时交作业，我有时请小王帮我做，实际上自己并没有学会。

乙：你这样是自欺欺人，应该向老师承认错误，并请老师辅导一下。

甲：那样老师和小王都会生我气的。

乙：知错改错不算错。你再这样下去，只会是错上加错，害了别人，也害了自己。

Quot. "等我老了，儿媳妇要是也学着我干，我会有什么好下场！大娘呀，你说我该怎么办呀？""人常说'知错能改不为错。'你把他奶奶接回家，问题不就解决了吗？"（杨锁田《春风》）

Cf. 一针不补，十针难缝/低头是水，回头是岸，及时挽救得一半/亡羊补牢未为迟/知过必改，便是圣贤/迷途知返，回头是岸/惑者知返，迷途不远

Var. 知错能改不为错/知错改错不算错，知错不改错中错

A fault confessed is half redressed

【义】承认错误就等于改了一半。

【解】做错了就要勇于承认。只有认识到错误才有利于迅速纠正。

【例】A：Brenda，I am sorry I forgot to give you the message from your boss yesterday. Here it is.

B：Oh，this was the message I was expecting. It was very important.

A：Gosh，I am terribly sorry I made such a mistake. I hope my forgetfulness has not created a serious problem.

B：I am sure everything will work out. Remember：**A fault confessed is half redressed**. I'll explain to my boss what happened.

A：Telling you the truth helps to correct the error I made yesterday. I feel a little better now.

【引】A fault confessed is half redressed，so I hope he will forgive us.（O'Donnell，*Xanadu Talisman*）

【参】A trouble shared is a trouble halved. / Open confession is good for the soul. / He who makes no mistake makes nothing.

【异】Confession of a fault makes half amends. / A fault confessed is half forgiven.

Zhīzúzhě chánɡ lè

知足者常乐

Voc. 知足 be content with one's lot，者-er，乐 happy

Lit. Those who are content with what they have are always happy.

Exp. It suggests that contentment brings happiness.

Ex. 甲：你看起来好像有点儿不高兴，怎么回事？

乙：我这次考试成绩不好。

甲：得了多少分？

乙：只得了八十五分。

甲：这个成绩不错嘛。知足者常乐，你应该高兴才对。

乙：我的目标是一百分，这样的成绩让我怎么高兴得起来？

Quot. 贵国俗话说得好：见好就收，知足者常乐。以先生的精明能干，年富力强，还愁日后不能飞黄腾达吗？（罗国士、刘迪华《黑水魂》）

Cf. 知足不辱，知止不殆

Var. 知足心常乐，能思身自安/知足者常乐，能忍者自安

Enough is as good as a feast

【义】能吃饱肚子和受到盛宴款待是一样的。

【解】比喻一个人是否感到幸福往往不在于生活水平的高低，而在于能否满足于现实。

【例】A：It seems you are unhappy. What's wrong?

B：I didn't do well in my exam.

A：What's your grade?

B：I've got a B.

A：Not bad. You should be happy for what you have got. Remember：**Enough is as good as a feast**.

B：Well, my goal is to get an A. How could I be happy for a B?

【引】I like sopranos up to a point, but when she sang three songs straight off, her voice began to grate on me. Enough is as good as a feast, as the saying goes. (R. Ridout & C. Witting, *English Proverbs Explained*, 1967)

【参】The poor are rich when they are satisfied. / He is not poor that has little, but he that desires more. / A man is not poor if he can laugh. / If you have bread, don't look for cake. / Contentment makes poor men rich; discontentment makes rich men poor. / Poor folks fare the best. / Safety lies in the middle course.

【异】Enough is great riches. / Enough of a good thing is plenty. / More than enough is too much.

Zhǐyào gōngfu shēn, tiě chǔ móchéng zhēn

只要功夫深，铁杵磨成针

Voc. 功夫 effort，铁杵 iron rod，磨 grind，针 needle

Lit. Constant grinding turns an iron rod into a needle.

Exp. Every task can be accomplished no matter how hard it is, as long as you are determined and make great efforts.

Ex. 甲：这门课真难，我恐怕及不了格了。

乙：你应该有毅力，坚持学习。别忘了，只要功夫深，铁杵磨成针。

甲：但是，我上的这门课是有机化学！太难懂了。

乙：相信我。只要你有坚定的信念，就可以克服任何障碍。

甲：好吧。我会狠下功夫，把这根铁杵磨成绣花针。

Quot. 爷爷鼓励他说："现在咱成主人了，没有文化不行啊，你应该好好学习。俗话说：'只要功夫深，铁杵磨成针'，你年纪还轻轻的，路子长着哪。"（姜树茂《渔岛怒潮》）

Cf. 只要不怕苦和难，搬倒天山也不难

Var. 钝铁磨成针，只要功夫深/钢梁磨成针，功到自然成/铁打房梁磨成针

Faith will move mountains

【义】信念能移山。

【解】无论怎样艰难的任务，只要下定决心，坚持不懈，就一定能完成。

【例】A：This class is so difficult. I am not sure I'll pass it.

B：Be persistent and keep studying. Remember：**Faith will move mountains**.

A：But this is organic chemistry! It is too hard to understand.

B：Trust me. When you believe hard enough，you can overcome any obstacle.

A：OK. I'll try to have a positive attitude and keep the faith that I'll eventually move this big mountain.

【引】Faith moves mountains，they say，and hope lights up our darkness. (C. Fremlin，*With No Crying*)

If mountains can be moved by faith，you can surely move your own legs! (S. Grand，*Beth Book*)

Zhǐyào xiān shàng chuán, zìrán xiān dào àn

只要先上船，自然先到岸

Voc. 上 get on，船 boat，自然 naturally，岸 shore

Lit. The first to get on a boat is the first to arrive on the shore.

Exp. Those who arrive or start early get a better choice or opportunity.

Ex. 甲：还看书呢？一起出去打球吧。
乙：我想早日通过 HSK，所以每天都得认真复习。
甲：明年再考也一样。
乙：只要先上船，自然先到岸。通过了 HSK，我就可以马上到中国留学了。

Quot. 虽说有命存焉，难以预定，“只要先上船，自然先上岸”。（文康《儿女英雄传》，第三十回）

Cf. 人勤春早/先下手为强，后下手遭殃/早起三先，后起三慌/马后炮，赶不到/隔夜的金子，比不上当日的铜

First come, first served

【义】谁先来就先给谁服务。

【解】表示先行动就先得到服务，就会有更多的选择和机会。

【例】A：Have you ever noticed how Uncle Bob is always the first in line for food?

B：Yes，I have. Why do you think that is?

A：Well，you know，**first come，first served**.

B：Oh，I remember that proverb. It means he who arrives first has the best choices.

A：That is exactly what I mean. Say，let's get in line behind Uncle Bob.

B：Let's go!

【引】Starting today，special benefit tickets for the May 24th celebration are available on a first-come first-served basis. (*New York Times*, 1983)

【参】The early bird catches the worm.

【异】It's first come，first served. / on a first-come first-served basis

Zhǐ shang huà de bǐng, kàn dé chī bu dé

纸上画的饼，看得吃不得

Voc. 饼 round flat cake

Lit. You can only see but can't eat the cake on paper.

Exp. Don't count on something you want unless it is actually here.

Ex. 甲：我想买辆新车。你有什么好建议？

乙：我当然喜欢今年的新车型。

甲：你知道，那辆旧车我早就开够了。我在公司干得不错，今年肯定拿大奖。

乙：但愿如此。但是纸上画的饼，看得吃不得。

甲：说不定你是对的。在拿到奖金以前我最好先别想着怎么花。说实话，我现在连买个新电脑的钱都不够。

Quot. "……将来社越办越好，猪喂得多，会常打牙祭。""将来还是纸上画的饼，看得吃不得。我这人是只看眼前的。"（周立波《山乡巨变》）

Cf. 做梦娶媳妇/竹篮打水一场空/望梅止渴渴难止，画饼充饥人更饥/画饼不充饥，望梅不止渴

Don't count your chickens before they're hatched

【义】小鸡雏没有孵化出来以前不要计算你会有多少只鸡。

【解】说明凡事在未取得结果以前，不应幻想并依赖于成功的结果。

【例】A：I am thinking about buying a new car. What kind of cars do you like?

B：Of course I like this year's new model.

A：Well, you know I have been doing well in my company, and I am quite sure that I will receive a big bonus this year. I really want to get rid of my old car.

B：I hope so. However, **don't count your chickens before they are hatched**.

A：Maybe you're right. I shouldn't count on the bonus before I actually receive it from my boss. To be honest, right now I don't even have enough money for a new computer.

【引】Mr. Smith hoped to be made manager before the end of the year and have his salary greatly increased. He started placing orders ... "Don't count your chickens before they're hatched," warned his wife. (R. Ridout & C. Witting, *English Proverbs Explained*, 1967)

【参】Never spend your money before you have it. / First catch your hare, then cook him. / Catch your bear before you sell its skin. / Don't shout until you are out of the woods. / There's many a slip between the cup and the lip.

【异】Never count your chickens before they are hatched. / Don't count your chickens before the eggs are laid. / No good counting the chickens before they're hatched. / Don't count your chickens before they hatch.

Zhòng guā dé guā, zhòng dòu dé dòu

种瓜得瓜，种豆得豆

Voc. 播种 sow，瓜 melon，豆 bean

Lit. Plant melons and you get melons, sow beans and you get beans.

Exp. The things you are doing determine the results you will get out of them.

Ex. 甲：真急人，我表哥进派出所了。

乙：为什么？

甲：他一直有小偷小摸的恶习，还以为别人抓不住他。这次他在商店里偷东西的时候被逮住了。

乙：你知道吗？这就叫种瓜得瓜，种豆得豆，这样的后果得他自己承担。

Quot. 俗话说："种瓜得瓜，种豆得豆。"播什么种子，自然就会有什么收获。（刘彦林《三月潮》）

Cf. 种了高粱不出谷子/种禾得稻，敬老得宝/种牡丹者得花，种蒺藜者得刺

Var. 种瓜须得瓜，种豆须得豆/种瓜得瓜，种粟得粟/种瓜得瓜，种豆得豆，谁家种仇谁家收

You reap what you sow

【义】你播种什么就收获什么。

【解】比喻做一件事所付出的努力与得到的结果是相联系的。

【例】A：I'm so upset. My cousin is now in jail.

B：Why is he in jail?

A：He always had a habit of pilfering. He never thought that he'd be caught. Finally he was caught for shoplifting.

B：You know, they say, "**You reap what you sow.**"

A：Yes, we all know our actions have consequences.

【引】"You should never have left them," said Irma, "As you sow, Praxis, so you reap." (F. Weldon, *Praxis*)

【参】What goes around, comes around. / You've made your bed, now lie in it.

【异】As you sow, so you reap. / They that sow the wind shall reap the whirlwind. / As we sow, we reap. / Reap as one has sown.

Zhòngrén shí chái huǒyàn gāo

众人拾柴火焰高

Voc. 拾柴 collect firewood，火焰 flame

Lit. The flames rise high when everybody adds fuel to it.

Exp. We can accomplish more as a group than one can by himself.

Ex. 甲：要是想有个好点儿的保险，那么我们最好一起向保险公司提出我们的请求。

乙：你以为保险公司会听我们的吗？我上次索赔就被他们拒绝了。

甲：我相信众人拾柴火焰高。要是大家都对现有的保险条例不满意，就得一起行动。单靠一个人提肯定什么用也没有。

丙：我同意。集体的力量比个人的力量大。我们开会讨论一下儿吧。最好把我们的要求写下来，大家签名以后再交给保险公司。这次说不定他们会听我们的。

Quot. 别着急，我说的是实际问题。俗话说得好，众人拾柴火焰高，大家起来斗争就有办法。（雪克《战斗的青春》）

Cf. 人心齐，泰山移/一根筷子容易断，一把筷子折不弯/独木不成林/三个臭皮匠，抵个诸葛亮

Var. 一人拾柴火不旺，众人拾柴火焰高

Union is strength

【义】团结就是力量。

【解】表示如果具有同样目标的人在一起共同努力，那么可以超过其中任何一个人的力量。

【例】A：If we want to have a better insurance policy, we had better get together and present our request to the company.

B：Do you think the insurance company is going to listen to us? My claim was rejected by the company last time.

A：I believe **union is strength**. If all of us are dissatisfied with the policy, we should act together. We won't get anywhere by requesting the change individually.

C：I agree. We can accomplish more as a union than we can if we act as individuals. Let's have a meeting to discuss about it. We can put down our demands and present them to the insurance company after signing it. Maybe they will listen to us this time.

【引】"Union is strength," and that is the only kind that can control the floods of such a great father of rivers (the Mississippi). (Robinson, *Letter 29 Dec. in Indiana History Collections*, *XXII*, 1936)

【参】United we stand, divided we fall. / There's safety in numbers. / A house divided against itself can't stand.

【异】In unity there is strength.

英文索引
Index of English Proverbs

A

B

C

D

参考书目
Bibliography

1. Simpson, John & Speake, Jennifer (1998) *The Concise Oxford Dictionary of Proverbs*, 3rd Edition. Oxford University Press.
2. Titelman, Gregory (1996) *Popular Proverbs & Sayings.* New York: Random House, Inc.
3. Ridout, Ronald & Witting, Clifford. (1967) *English Proverbs Explained.* London: Heinemann Educational Books Ltd.
4. Cordry, Harold (1997) *The Multicultural Dictionary of Proverbs.* McFarland & Company, Inc., Publishers.
5. 温瑞政、王树山、沈慧云（主编）（1999）《谚语》，北京：语文出版社。
6. 徐宗才、应俊玲（1998）《俗语词典》，北京：商务印书馆。
7. 文桥出版社（1998）《英汉谚语词典》，台北：文桥出版社。
8. 温瑞政（主编）（1989）《中国俗语大词典》，上海：上海辞书出版社。

鸣谢

汉、英谚语浩如烟海，靠个人的收集难以反映全貌。本书的编写借助了大量的工具书、参考书和书刊报章。因此，编者对在书后参考书目中所列的作者和他们的著作表示感谢。为了反映谚语使用的真实面貌，编者还邀请 Dr. Sara Woods，Mr. Steven Chamberlin，Ms. Melissa Coultes 等提供了许多英语谚语的用例。书中配合谚语的插图由杜肖牧女士绘制，尹惠莹女士帮助整理索引并打印了全书初稿。Ms. Katherine、A. Walker 校读了全书的英文部分。我的许多同事、学生也对本书的编写投入了极大的兴趣和支持。在此一并致谢。

北京语言大学出版社在本书的编辑、修改和出版过程中给予了大量的支持和帮助，特致谢忱。

Acknowledgement

It is certainly impossible to give an overall introduction to both Chinese and English proverbs by an individual's collection, since the content is so rich and colorful. Therefore, many reference books and articles were used in the preparation of this book. This book wouldn't have been completed without the availability of those materials. I would like to take this opportunity to acknowledge the consultation of the books mentioned in the *Bibliography* with respectful appreciation. To show the usage of the English proverbs, I also invited Dr. Sara Woods, Mr. Steven Chamberlin, Ms. Melissa Coultes and others to provide examples in real language situations. Ms. Du Xiaomu drew the pictures to associate with and illustrate the proverbs. Ms. Yin Huiying spent many hours helping with the index and typing the draft of the book. Ms katherine A. Walker thoroughly proofread the English texts. Many of my colleagues and students also showed their support to this book with great interest. I am indebted to all of them, and I would like to give my deep appreciation for their contributions.

My thanks also go to Beijing Language & Culture University Press for their generous and consistent support in editing, designing and printing this book. It wouldn't be possible to publish this book without their help.

外国人说熟语

Chinese Idiomatic Phrases for Foreign Students

徐宗才 应俊玲 编著

适用对象：中高级水平的汉语学习者

注释文种：英文

定价：25.00 元

ISBN 978-7-5619-1048-1

本书选取了最常用的汉语惯用语、成语、俗语557条，每个熟语配1-2组情景对话，对话后附有多种搭配形式，帮助母语非汉语的学习者通过学说现成的句子，逐渐熟悉、掌握汉语熟语。

This book selects 557 locutions, idioms and proverbs that are the most commonly used ones in Chinese. For each idiom there is one or two groups of situational conversations with various collocation forms attached for learning. It helps the non-native Chinese speakers gradually get familiar with and master Chinese idioms by learning to speak ready sentences.

听故事 学成语

Learning through Listening: An Introduction to Chinese Proverbs and Their Origins

马盛静恒 编著

适用对象：中高级水平的汉语学习者

注释文种：英文

定价：25.00 元

ISBN 978-7-5619-0971-3

本书选择了15个常用成语编写故事，语言浅显易懂，不但可以训练学习者的听说读写能力，还能帮助他们更进一步地了解中国文化。课文简繁体对照，注有拼音，另有成语用法举例、生词注解及练习等内容。随书赠CD一盘。

This book includes 15 commonly-used idiomatic expressions and tells interesting stories about them in simple language. Reading these stories can not only improve learners' listening and speaking skills, but also help them understand Chinese culture better. All texts are printed in both traditional and simplified Chinese. Example sentences, illustrations, explanation to new words, and exercises are also given in the book.

汉语口语习惯用语教程

A Course in Chinese Colloquial Idioms

沈建华 编著

适用对象：中高级水平的汉语学习者

注释文种：英文

定价：31.00 元

ISBN 978-7-5619-1192-1

本书通过20个对话场景，帮助学习者了解、掌握500个常用的汉语口语习惯用语，提高其汉语表达能力。另配有录音CD和磁带。

In order to help foreign learners understand the meanings and usages of common Chinese colloquial idioms, the compiler collects some commonly-used oral expressions and designs 20 situational dialogues. Brief explanations, appropriate example sentences and exercises are provided. With this book, learners will get to know 500 commonly-used Chinese oral expressions and improve their Chinese speaking skills. Accompanied are audio CDs and cassettes.

汉语口语常用句

Basic Chinese Sentences

柳燕梅 翟艳 编著

适用对象：初级汉语水平、掌握800-1000词的汉语学习者

注释文种：英文/俄文

定价：22.00 元

ISBN 978-7-5619-1166-2

本书是为外国人编写的生活用语手册，以日常生活、校园生活为背景，简便实用。全书以功能、情景为纲，分为上下两篇，包含近千句生活用语，查阅方便。

本书有英文、俄文两种注释本，另配有录音CD。

This pamphlet is compiled for foreigners to learn daily life expressions. Setting in daily life and school life, it is simple, convenient and of great practical use. The book is divided into two chapters, which are then subdivided according to different language functions and situations. It includes nearly one thousand daily life expressions and is convenient for referring to. It has annotations in both English and Russian. An audio CD is included.

作为国内外知名的对外汉语教学与研究专业出版社，为给广大读者和合作伙伴提供更优质、高效的服务，北京语言大学出版社于2006年9月和12月推出了全新改版的中文和英文网站：

◇ 已发布2000余种语言教学类产品，产品信息不断更新；提供快速检索和产品预览功能。

◇ 支持国际信用卡在线支付和DHL全球快递等多种支付和配送渠道，为用户在线订购图书及音像制品提供极大便利。

◇ 与北语社教材配套的教学资源，如教案、课件、试题、听力资源等也正在网站上不断丰富，为使用北语社产品的教师、学生和经销商提供有力的支持和增值服务。

◇ 已建立快速响应客户服务机制，网站的客服电子信箱、访客留言、产品评论及回复等功能构成了出版社与用户交流互动的平台。

北京语言大学出版社网站

WWW.BLCUP.COM

Open a window into Chinese language and culture

◇ More than 2000 CSL (Chinese as a Second Language) and other foreign language titles are available on BLCUP website.

◇ Blcup.com offers various payment methods. It's easy and safe to make payment online via a VISA or MASTER card.

◇ With DHL Express Courier and other delivery options, Blcup.com can ship to virtually any address in the world.

◇ We appreciate customers' feedback and provide quick response service. If you have a comment, query or support request, please leave a message on *Contact us* page of BLCUP website.